LIFE IN A MEDIEVAL
ABBEY

Tony McAleavy

ENCHANTED LION BOOKS
NEW YORK

CONTENTS

DAILY LIFE

From the early hours of the morning until dusk, the lives of monks and nuns centred on the daily round of services held in the abbey church. Other activities, from manuscript illumination to caring for the sick, were similarly dedicated to God.

THE ORIGINS OF MONASTIC LIFE

How and why did monasticism first come to Britain? The thriving monasteries of the Middle Ages had austere origins in the Middle East. Centuries later, monasticism was brought to Britain by successive waves of invaders: Celts, Saxons, Vikings and Normans.

First American Edition published in 2003 by
Enchanted Lion Books, 239 Central Park West, New York, NY, 10024
Copyright © 1998 English Heritage
Edited by Kate Jeffrey   Designed by Martin Atcherley
Picture Researcher: Dana Phillips
Historical Consultant: Brian Davison
All Rights Reserved
Printed in the European Union by Snoeck-Ducaju & Zoon
A CIP record for this book is available
from the Library of Congress
ISBN 1-59270-006-3
Front cover illustration: St. Dunstan as a monk, with angel and devil,
from a twelfth-century stained glass window, Canterbury Cathedral

MONASTERIES IN THE MEDIEVAL WORLD

Even at the heart of an abbey, the secular world was never far away. From the giving of alms to the advising of kings, monks and nuns played a crucial role in the economic, political and cultural life of the country.

DECLINE AND FALL

By the sixteenth century abbeys and monasteries had lost much of their influence and power. The dissolution gave Henry VIII an excuse to seize their wealth while advancing his personal ends; but despite the destruction, the monastic heritage lives on to this day.

INTRODUCTION

FOR NEARLY 1000 YEARS monasteries dominated the landscape of England and the lives of countless English people. Men and women who took religious vows committed themselves to a unique way of life: cloistered within the abbey, they submitted to the austere surroundings and rigorous discipline prescribed by their order. For many, the knowledge that they were serving Christ was sufficient reward; and in a world of poverty and hardship, the hope of salvation in the life to come must have been a powerful spur. Not all monks and nuns were motivated by piety alone. Throughout the Middle Ages a fascinating variety of people joined the monasteries, from saints and statesmen to rogues and runaways. Life within the abbey centred on the church, where, following the teachings of the Italian monk, St Benedict, monks and nuns spent much of their day praising God and carrying out an arduous round of religious ritual. These same monks and nuns made an incalculable contribution to the cultural life of the country. The early medieval monasteries acted as beacons of scholarship and artistic endeavour in an otherwise dark, unlettered world.

Yet although for centuries the monasteries must have seemed a fixed part of the medieval landscape, their story in Britain has a beginning, and, dramatically, an end. While the first part of this book aims to give a sense of what it was like to live in an abbey at the height of the Middle Ages, the second travels back in time to explain how monasticism came into being and how it was established in Britain. The first monks lived as hermits in the Middle Eastern desert in the fourth century. Later, St Benedict created a model for monastic life which was influential throughout Europe. Britain was also subject to a different influence: Celtic monks led missions to northern England

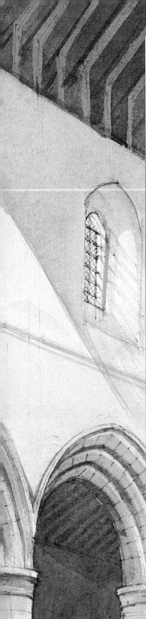

and there established their own distinct brand of monasticism. The combination of these two traditions led to a particularly creative flowering of monasticism in Anglo-Saxon England, but these early monasteries were brought to a violent close by the Viking raids of the eighth century and were only fully revived with the Norman Conquest. Shortly afterwards monks from Burgundy brought to Britain a radical, reforming movement: the Cistercians went on to become perhaps the most vigorous order of all.

Abbeys and monasteries did not exist in isolation, and the book goes on to explore their relationship with the wider world. As institutions they offered charity to the poor and hospitality to visitors. Collectively, monasteries owned a large proportion of the land of England. Monks and nuns could be energetic landowners and powerful politicians. They were not without their enemies and periodically came into conflict with jealous kings and rebellious tenants.

By the time the Middle Ages drew to a close the monasteries had lost their leading position in society. In its final part, the book shows how in some monasteries standards had lapsed while in others monastic idealism remained strong. The complex world of medieval monasticism was swept away during the religious storms of the sixteenth-century Reformation. Under Henry VIII all the monasteries of England were closed and their inmates dispersed. Yet the energy and power of medieval monks and nuns lives on in the monastic buildings that survive them. Despite the devastation of the sixteenth century and the subsequent ravages of time, much of the architectural heritage of monasticism can still be enjoyed by visitors today. This book is intended to bring the abbey ruins to life, and, by doing so, to demonstrate the rich diversity of medieval monasticism.

Main picture: An imaginative reconstruction of the church at Cleeve Abbey, Somerset. Above right: An angel looks down to earth, an illustration from a thirteenth-century preaching manual

At the heart of a strict monastery was the church. Here monks and nuns spent much of their time in communal prayer, following an established timetable. Even more mundane matters were strictly regulated: talking, eating, washing and sleeping. Monks and nuns created some of the most magnificent works of art of the Middle Ages. Many of the greatest writers and thinkers also belonged to religious orders.

WHO'S WHO IN A MEDIEVAL ABBEY?

Most medieval abbeys followed a set of rules laid down by the sixth-century monk, St Benedict. Benedict originally prescribed these rules for his own monastery at Monte Cassino in Italy, but by the Middle Ages they had become influential throughout western Europe. The Rule of St Benedict described a fairly simple community life in which monks lived together as a large family, presided over by the abbot. During the course of the Middle Ages, however, monasteries became more complex organisations and different tasks were assigned to different monks or nuns. In particular, a wide division often developed between the abbot and the rest of the monastery. Whereas at first an abbot or abbess was expected to sleep in the common dormitory, by 1150 this had become extremely uncommon and the head of the house usually lodged in separate quarters. Their financial arrangements were also separately managed, and some of the estates of the monastery were seen as their exclusive preserve. In most large monasteries there also developed a gulf between the ordinary monks and nuns and the 'obedientiaries', senior members of the community who held powerful posts in the running of the monastery. The obedientiaries were allowed to miss church sevices in order to carry out administrative duties and sometimes went outside the abbey on business. In the later Middle Ages they too tended to move away from the dormitory and set up their own apartments elsewhere in the abbey.

The roles described in the following account are based on a male Benedictine monastery and give a sense of the wide range of activities required of the monks. Depending on their size, nunneries had a very similar personnel. The quotations all come from a guide to monastic life written in the late eleventh century by Lanfranc, the archbishop of Canterbury.

CHOIR MONKS

Those who did not hold office as obedientiaries were known as 'choir' or 'cloister' monks. They were expected to carry out the full round of prayers and church services, whereas obedientiaries had permission to be absent. Nunneries were orgainsed along similar lines. *Above:* Cloister nuns of the Franciscan order chant the psalms in church, an activity that would have taken up much of their waking day.

THE PRIOR was the abbot's deputy and was in charge of discipline. In large monasteries there were sometimes also several sub-priors:

❖ Saving the reverence due to the abbot, the prior is to be honoured above the other servants of God's house. He takes precedence in the choir and chapter and refectory. If the abbot be far away he may depose from office those whom he learns to be handling their business in a way contrary to the profit of the monastery. When he enters the chapter house all rise and stand.

THE NOVICES AND MASTER OF NOVICES. The master of novices oversaw new recruits. As well as maintaining discipline it was his duty to ensure that novices learned by heart the complicated Latin prayers that were chanted in the choir:

❖ The older boys shall sit apart from one another. In the afternoon they shall not read or write or do any work but shall simply rest. If necessity causes them to rise at night, they shall first rouse their masters, and then lighting a candle, they shall go with them to relieve themselves. They shall not speak with one another unless a master is present to hear what is being said.

THE ALMONER was in charge of the distribution of alms (charity) to the poor:

❖ He shall take great pains to discover where may lie those sick and weakly persons who are without means of sustenance. Entering a house he shall speak kindly and comfort the sick man, and offer him the best of what he has.

THE GUEST-MASTER supervised the guest-house and was responsible for offering hospitality to visitors. The Rule of St Benedict required monks to provide hospitality, a service which was fully exploited by members of the royal family and nobility, who relied on monasteries to provide lodgings during their travels:

> The brother who is appointed to receive guests should have ready in the guest-house beds, chairs, tables, towels, cloths, tankards, plates, spoons, basins and suchlike. Whoever wishes to speak with the abbot, prior or any monk shall use the guest-master as his ambassador.

THE INFIRMARER looked after the 'infirmary' or sick-house. Here the strict dietary rules of the monastery were relaxed. In the early Middle Ages monks were often distinguished doctors. *Above:* A Benedictine monk lies on his bed in the infirmary.

> Every day after Compline he shall sprinkle holy water over all the beds of the sick. He himself shall place before the sick brethren all the dishes prepared for them.

THE CANTOR OR PRECENTOR was in charge of the chanting of prayers in the abbey choir. He also had responsibility for the library and the scholarly work of the monks:

> Whenever anyone has to read or chant anything in the church the cantor shall, if need be, hear him go over his task before he performs it in public. He takes care of all the books of the house and has them in his keeping.

THE CELLARER was a particularly powerful figure. He managed the purchase of all food and drink, fuel and other routine expenses. *Above:* A cellarer, with his keys, tests the drink of the abbey.

> He shall provide utensils for the cellar and the kitchen, and flagons and tankards and other vessels for the refectory. He should be the father of the whole community, and should have a care for the sound and still more for the sick.

THE CHAMBERLAIN was responsible for all the monks' clothing. He also supervised bedding, bathing and shaving:

> He sees to the glazing and repairing of the dormitory windows. To brethren about to go on journey he shall give capes, gaiters and spurs. Once a year he causes the straw to be removed in all the beds.

THE SACRIST looked after the church and its furnishings. He was responsible for vestments, ornaments and lighting, and in some abbeys also took charge of any building work. *Above:* This reconstruction illustration shows the sacrist at work at the Cistercian abbey at Cleeve, Somerset.

> His task is to ring the bells, or to instruct others how they are to be rung. He distributes candles. He takes charge of burials. It is his task twice a week to wash the chalices.

LAY BROTHERS. The Cistercians greatly developed the class of monks known as 'conversi' or lay brothers. These were men from a poor background who were usually illiterate. They did much of the manual labour needed on the farms or 'granges' of the abbey.

LAY SERVANTS. From the earliest days monks made use of paid labour by 'lay servants' who were not part of the monastic community. The number of lay servants increased during the Middle Ages as monasteries became more complex, and monks and nuns did less manual labour. The Cistercians reduced the number of lay servants, but were unable to dispense entirely with non-monastic help. *Right:* In this manuscript illustration a lay brother, in his brown habit, swings an axe at the base of the tree, while a lay servant performs the more dangerous work in the upper branches.

7

A TIMETABLE OF WORSHIP

The Rule of St Benedict set out how prayers should be conducted in the abbey church. The heart of the daily services was the chanted recital of the 'psalter' (prayers from the Book of Psalms). The whole of the Book of Psalms was recited during the course of each week. This round of daily prayer was called the 'opus Dei' – the Work of God. Benedict had stated that there should be eight services or 'offices', comprising a night service, later known as Matins, and seven daytime offices: Lauds, Prime, Terce, Sext, None, Vespers and Compline. The decision to organise prayers in this way was based on two statements in the Psalms: 'At midnight I rose to give praise to thee' and 'Seven times a day have I given praise to thee'.

Benedict assigned particular psalms to particular services. His instructions contained some homely touches. The first prayer of the first service of the day was to be chanted slowly 'in order that all may assemble in time'. He also stated that monks should sleep dressed and ready for prayer:

> Being clothed they will thus always be ready, and rising at the signal without any delay may hasten to forestall one another to the Work of God. When they rise for the Work of God, let them gently encourage one another, on account of the excuses to which the sleepy are addicted.

Benedict recommended that the timetable not be too burdensome; the eight services should be short enough to allow time for study and manual labour. He looked back with admiration to the time of the first monks of the desert, commenting that the pioneers of monasticism recited the psalms so quickly that many of them were able to complete all 150 every day. As time passed the conduct of the services became more elaborate and time-consuming. New prayers and repetitions were added. The eucharistic service of the mass, performed only on Sundays in Benedict's day, became daily, and then a second celebration was added. This tendency to ever more complex liturgy reached its height in the elaborate ritual of the Cluniac monasteries.

BELOW *Two monks sharing a book. Benedictines and Cluniacs came to spend so much time in church that the opportunities for private reading were limited*

A DAY OF PRAYER

In the tenth century the day in winter started at about two o'clock in the morning. The monks went to the church using special 'night stairs' that linked the dormitory to the church. With some brief pauses, the offices of Matins, Lauds and Prime kept the monks in the church until nearly seven o'clock. They then had an opportunity for reading until eight. They went back briefly to the dormitory and washed before returning to the church for Terce and the first mass of the day. From nine o'clock for half an hour the community met in the chapter house to discuss business and discipline. Afterwards the monks performed work of various kinds. At about half-past twelve they undertook the office of Sext, followed by a second, more formal celebration of the mass. After the mass, the office of None was recited. At about two o'clock in the afternoon the monks ate dinner, their only meal of the day in winter. Between three and five o'clock in the afternoon there was a second period of reading or work. Vespers were chanted, a brief break and a drink were taken, and the final service of Compline took place until about seven o'clock. The monks then went to bed.

ABOVE *Benedictine monks at the eucharistic service of the mass. Some orders, such as the Carthusians, sought to put a greater emphasis on private prayer*

BELOW *A 'cresset' lamp from Furness Abbey in Cumbria. The wicks floated in oil in the depressions. It probably stood in the dormitory and was used to light the way to the church at night*

A RETURN TO SIMPLICITY

This intensive day of formal prayer was even more time-consuming on the numerous feast days. In Cluniac houses on such occasions most of the waking day was spent in church. Not all monks approved of this almost constant cycle of public prayer. The establishment of the Cistercian and Carthusian orders was based on a belief that excessive amounts of time in church could be a barrier to spiritual development. St Bernard, the great Cistercian abbot of Clairvaux, was also critical of the way in which Cluniac houses used expensively decorated vestments and chalices in their services:

> Candlesticks as tall as trees, great masses of bronze of exquisite workmanship, dazzling with precious stones, what is the point of all of this? Will it melt a sinner's heart? O vanity of vanities – no, insanity rather than vanity.

The Cistercians altered the timetable and provided more time for study, work and private prayer. They insisted on a new simplicity in the decoration of their churches and a reduction in the elaborate ritual of the services. The Cistercians also rejected the idea that members of the public should witness their prayers. All Cistercian abbeys had a chapel built near the great gate as a place of worship for the lay people. The Carthusians too kept the public at a distance and altered the timetable in a radical way. They required their monks to undertake most of the offices of the day through solitary prayer in their cells. As a result the Carthusian church was an extremely small building compared to the great Benedictine monastic churches. The Carthusian lifestyle represented a return to the spirit of the first hermit monks in Egypt.

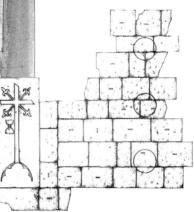

In addition to prayer, monks and nuns also spent time on more mundane matters. In strict communities, talking, eating, washing and sleeping were as closely regulated as were the church services. The Rule of St Benedict discouraged unnecessary conversation. In the refectory a rule of silence usually applied and this led to the use of elaborate forms of sign language.

Diet was a cause of great controversy. St Benedict had prescribed two meals a day in summer, but only one in winter. Reformers often struggled to ensure a strict adherence to this rule. Meat was forbidden except for the sick, but by 1250 it was common for monks to have meat as a treat when dining with the abbot or in the infirmary (irrespective of whether or not they were ill).

Ritual washing took place daily but bathing was less frequent; in the eleventh century Lanfranc expected his monks to bathe five times a year:

ABOVE *Sculpture from the lavabo or monks' washing-place at Wenlock Priory, Shropshire. The carvings date from the late twelfth century. The use of such elaborate decoration for a wash-basin indicates the importance of washing in the monks' daily round*

◆ The brethren shall, when shaved, take their change of clothes and go to the place where the baths are prepared, and there, taking off their clothes in due order as they do in the dormitory, they shall enter the bathing place as directed, and letting down the curtain that hangs before them they shall sit in silence in the bath. If anyone needs anything let him signal for it quietly, and a servant lifting the veil shall quickly take him what he wants and return at once. When he has finished washing himself, he shall not stay longer for pleasure but shall rise and dress and put on his shoes as he does in the dormitory, and having washed his hands shall return to the cloister.

BELOW *This remarkable plan of about 1160 shows the monastic buildings of Canterbury Cathedral Priory and its system of sanitation. Parts of the system are still in use today. This was the abbey for which Lanfranc had laid down rules and regulations in the late eleventh century.*

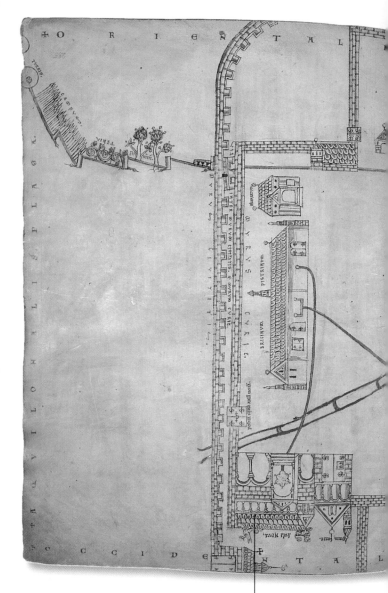

LEFT *Reconstruction drawing of the cloisters of Tintern Abbey in the thirteenth century, showing the Cistercian monks performing ritual washing before entering the refectory. Washing of this kind was part of the daily round in both Cistercian and Benedictine houses. Monks also took regular baths*

THE GUEST-HOUSE
Hospitality had been an important part of the Benedictine life since the time of Benedict. Important visitors expected to receive hospitality at a great Benedictine house. Close to the guest-house is a large, opulent

hall for the entertainment of guests; it is marked on the plan as 'aula nova', the new hall. In this area there are a number of other buildings including the main kitchen, the refectory, a brewhouse, bakery and bath-house.

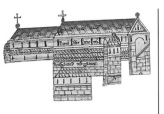

THE INFIRMARY BUILDINGS. *The plan shows a whole complex of buildings linked to the infirmary, including a chapel. All monks regularly visited the infirmary for periodic blood-letting, after which they spent two or three days convalescing. This was seen by many as a welcome holiday and break from routine. Jocelin of Brakelond, of Bury St Edmunds Abbey, talked about 'the time of blood-letting, when the cloister monks tend to reveal the secrets of their heart and to chat with each other'.*

ABOVE *An artist's impression of the refectory of Denny Abbey in Cambridge-shire in the fifteenth century. This was a female Franciscan house. Here one sister reads from a religious text, while the others eat in silence*

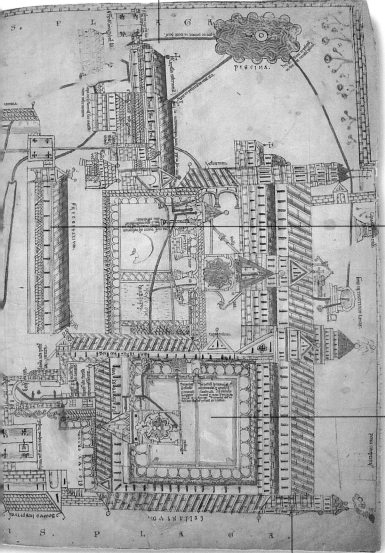

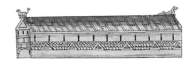

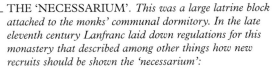

THE 'NECESSARIUM'. *This was a large latrine block attached to the monks' communal dormitory. In the late eleventh century Lanfranc laid down regulations for this monastery that described among other things how new recruits should be shown the 'necessarium':*

> And he shall be taken beyond the dormitory, and the cells shown him to which he is to repair when nature's way demand it, and he shall be told how to bear himself seemly there in sitting and departing, and how to satisfy the demands of nature with modesty.

THE CLOISTER. *At Canterbury this courtyard surrounded by a covered walkway was placed to the north of the monastic church, though this was atypical. More usually it was to the south, so that the alley closest to the church received the most sunlight and was the place where monks carried out their scholarly work. The eastern alley was traditionally where novices were instructed. The design of the cloister was more suited to a Mediterranean climate than to the cool British weather. At the time that this plan was made, the cloister at Canterbury would have been unglazed and unheated, making work difficult in the winter months.*

THE CATHEDRAL CHURCH. *About 100 monks were members of the Cathedral Priory in the mid-twelfth century. Some of them witnessed the martyrdom of Thomas Becket in the church in 1170. Medieval churches were often destroyed by fire: the choir of the church depicted here was burned down in 1174.*

During the early Middle Ages the idea of distinct religious orders was unknown. Most monasteries were entirely independent of each other. They followed the Rule of St Benedict but did not see themselves as part of a Benedictine order. A monk or nun was a member of a particular monastery, rather than an international organisation. This began to change with the Cluniac reforms of the tenth century. The abbey of Cluny founded other monasteries, which were not seen as separate abbeys but as an extension of the original house. Wherever he lived a Cluniac monk swore obedience to the abbot of Cluny.

The development of the idea of a religious 'order' was taken a stage further by the Cistercians. Apart from the first Cistercian abbey at Cîteaux, each abbey was founded by monks from a 'mother house'. Thus, monks from Cîteaux founded Clairvaux, and monks from Clairvaux established the English abbey at Rievaulx. The abbot of a mother house had the right and duty to oversee and inspect standards in each daughter house. Cistercian abbots were also obliged to take part in an annual meeting at Cîteaux. These arrangements meant that Cistercians were part of a disciplined order with identical customs in each of hundreds of abbeys across Europe.

The idea of commitment to an order rather than to a specific community was taken further by St Francis and St Dominic, the founding fathers of the friars. Unlike older orders of monks, the first friars were not bound to any one monastery, but travelled from place to place preaching and begging. They saw themselves as members of an international and highly cosmopolitan organisation. There was often intense rivalry between different religious orders. As new orders developed leading members of existing orders felt threatened. Fashions in religious life deprived long-established communities of talented recruits. As new orders emerged and won a reputation for sanctity, they often secured gifts and patronage at the expense of the older orders.

ABOVE *All the orders were dedicated to imitating and serving Christ. This illustration, by Matthew Paris of St Albans, shows a Benedictine monk carrying a large crucifix during a procession*

*c.*515 BENEDICTINES

Benedictines were also known as 'black monks' because of the colour of their habits. They traced their origins back to the work of St Benedict, an Italian monk of the early sixth century, who described the monastic life in a highly detailed Rule. The English Benedictine houses included some of the wealthiest and most powerful monasteries of the medieval period, such as Glastonbury and St Albans. Uniquely, some English Benedictine abbey churches were also cathedrals.

910 CLUNIACS

Cluniacs derived their name from the abbey of Cluny in Burgundy. The order was distinguished by its emphasis on the most elaborate church ceremonial. Cluniacs were highly regarded in the tenth and eleventh centuries because of this dedication to formal prayer and liturgy. So much of their time was devoted to church services that they were unable to perform any manual work and relatively little study.

1084 CARTHUSIANS

Carthusians were named after their first monastery, La Grande Chartreuse, in the mountains near Grenoble in eastern France. Each English Carthusian abbey was known as a Charterhouse. The Carthusians attempted to revive some of the spirit of the first hermits in the Egyptian desert. The monks lived in small houses, or cells, around a cloister and spent much of their time in solitary prayer and work. Throughout the Middle Ages they retained a reputation for great strictness. *Left:* A Carthusian monk reads outside his house.

1098 CISTERCIANS

Cistercians wore white habits, giving rise to their alternative name, 'white monks'. The order began as an attempt to reform Benedictine monasticism by following more closely the Rule of St Benedict. The early Cistercians had charismatic leaders, including the Englishman Stephen Harding and the Burgundian Bernard of Clairvaux – both of whom became saints after their deaths. The Cistercians were particularly devoted to the Virgin Mary and each abbey, with few exceptions, was dedicated to her. Many idealistic men and women were attracted to the Cistercian way of life in the twelfth century. Later, some Cistercian houses became extremely wealthy.

1120 KNIGHTS TEMPLAR
1120 KNIGHTS HOSPITALLERS

The Crusades led to the foundation of military orders. In addition to taking monastic vows of poverty, chastity and obedience, the Knights Templar and Knights Hospitallers were members of an armed force which carried out military service in conflicts with Islam, and escorted groups of pilgrims visiting the Holy Land. There was considerable rivalry between the two orders. The Templars were suppressed in 1312 and the Hospitallers took over most of their property.

REGULAR CANONS

The 'regular canons' lived in a community and followed a daily rule. Unlike many other monastic groups, however, they regarded service to local people as part of their calling. Augustinians, Premonstratensians and Gilbertines are all examples of canons.

1100 AUGUSTINIANS

The Augustinians followed a modified version of the monastic life based loosely on the teachings of the great fifth-century bishop, St Augustine of Hippo.

1121 PREMONSTRATENSIANS

The Premonstratensians were followers of the saintly Norbert of Prémontré, a friend of Bernard of Clairvaux. As well as following a programme of daily formal prayer, regular canons worked as parish priests and bishops and sometimes ran hospitals.

1131 GILBERTINES

The Gilbertines were the only medieval religious order that was exclusively English. They were founded by a Lincolnshire priest named Gilbert of Sempringham. This unusual order established 'double houses' in which both men and women were members of the same monastery. The majority of members were nuns following the Rule of St Benedict. However, male lay brothers undertook the manual labour, and male canons led in acts of worship.

FRIARS

A great new wave of religious enthusiasm swept Europe in the thirteenth century. Many sought to imitate Christ by joining the new communities of friars (see p.54). *Left:* This late fourteenth-century illustration shows four friars together with two devils!

1210 FRANCISCAN FRIARS

The Italian St Francis urged his followers to adopt a life of complete poverty. The earliest Franciscans moved about the world preaching and surviving by begging. They soon played an important part in the new universities as teachers. Despite the commitment of their founder to absolute poverty, the order eventually acquired substantial property and wealth. In England Franciscans were known as 'grey friars'.

1215 POOR CLARES

Each of the male orders of friars had a female counterpart. Church law forbade women from preaching and the female orders lived a more traditionally monastic life in an enclosed community. In England the most popular order was that of the Franciscan nuns or Poor Clares. They were founded by St Clare, a friend of St Francis.

1216 DOMINICAN FRIARS

Besides Francis, there was another great leader of the new orders, the Spaniard St Dominic. Dominic placed a particular emphasis on the importance of preaching, and the official name of his followers was the Order of Preachers. Dominicans were popularly known as 'black friars'.

1220 CARMELITE FRIARS
1255 AUGUSTINIAN FRIARS

These two smaller orders of friars placed a strong emphasis on solitary prayer; some of their members lived as hermits.

JOINING AN ABBEY

From the time of St Benedict through until the twelfth century there were two major sources of recruitment: children who were pledged to the monastic life by their parents, and young adults who chose to enter a monastery. In addition, some people became monks and nuns much later in life. Child recruits were known as 'oblates' or the 'children of the monastery'. They were free to leave until they took solemn vows as young adults.

Different methods of recruitment are neatly illustrated by the life of the historian, Orderic Vitalis. Orderic came from Shrewsbury but was sent away to the monastery of St Evroul in Normandy and never saw his family again. His father helped found a monastery in Shrewsbury and spent his own last years there as a monk. In the early twelfth century Orderic described how his father had given him as an oblate at the age of ten:

ABOVE *The tonsure or ritual shaving of the head of a new recruit. The tonsure was a symbolic way of showing that a person had joined a monastery. Later the recruit would take solemn vows promising a life-long commitment to life as a monk*

> My father, Odeler, wept as he gave me, a weeping child to Rainald the monk, and sent me into exile for your [Christ's] love – nor ever after saw me. A small boy did not presume to contradict his father, but I obeyed him in all things, since he promised me that I should possess paradise with the innocent. And so I left my country, my parents, all my kindred and my friends. At ten years old I crossed the Channel, and came, an exile, to Normandy, knowing no one, known to none. Like Joseph in Egypt, I heard a tongue I knew not. Yet by your grace I found among the strangers every kindness and friendship.

By the early twelfth century the oblate system was in decline and most recruits were adults. The first Cistercians vigorously rejected the practice, insisting that no one beneath the age of sixteen should be allowed to join their monasteries. Soon afterwards the custom disappeared in the Benedictine monasteries.

VOCATION OR CAREER?

The motives for joining a monastery were, doubtless, varied. Some, such as the first Cistercians, had a powerful sense of religious calling or vocation.

For others, family expectations may have been as important. Many nuns probably regarded the religious life as a career, almost the only one open to upper-class women other than marriage and motherhood. The chronicle of St Albans Abbey gives us a rare insight into the motives of a particular monk in the twelfth century. Before taking holy orders Geoffrey was a teacher at a school in Dunstable. He organised a miracle play in honour of St Katharine and borrowed a number of priceless copes (vestments) from the abbey as costumes. Then his house in Dunstable burned down and the vestments were destroyed. Mortified, and unable to pay for their replacement, Geoffrey offered himself to the abbey as a sacrifice to God. He went on to become abbot.

Medieval monks and nuns usually came from the wealthier section of society. Even in the poorest of nunneries many sisters were members of aristocratic or gentle families. There is virtually no evidence of women from a poor background becoming nuns. One major barrier to poor men and women joining a monastery was the expectation that novices would bring with them money or land as a gift when joining. This expectation is revealed in many medieval wills, such as this from Lincoln in 1345:

> I bequeath to the daughter of John de Playce, my brother, 100 shillings in silver, for an aid towards making her a nun in one of the houses of Wickham, Yedingham or Muncton.

RUNAWAYS

Once monks and nuns had taken their final vows they were bound to stay in their abbey for life. Some clearly regretted their decision because there are many records of runaways (known as 'apostates'). Monasteries were often energetic in their pursuit of runaways and could use the law to enforce their return:

> One brother John Bengeworthe, a monk, who had been imprisoned for his ill desert, brake prison and went into apostasy, taking with him a nun of Godstow, but he has now been brought back to the monastery and is still doing penance.
> *(Records of Eynsham Abbey, 1445)*

ABOVE *Stained glass from Canterbury showing monks at prayer. By choosing to enter a monastery monks committed themselves to a life of prayer and penance*

ABOVE *The robing of a novice. New recruits put away their worldly clothes to indicate their rejection of life outside the monastery*

BELOW *Not all recruits were suited to life in a monastery. Here an erring Benedictine monk and a lady are punished in the stocks*

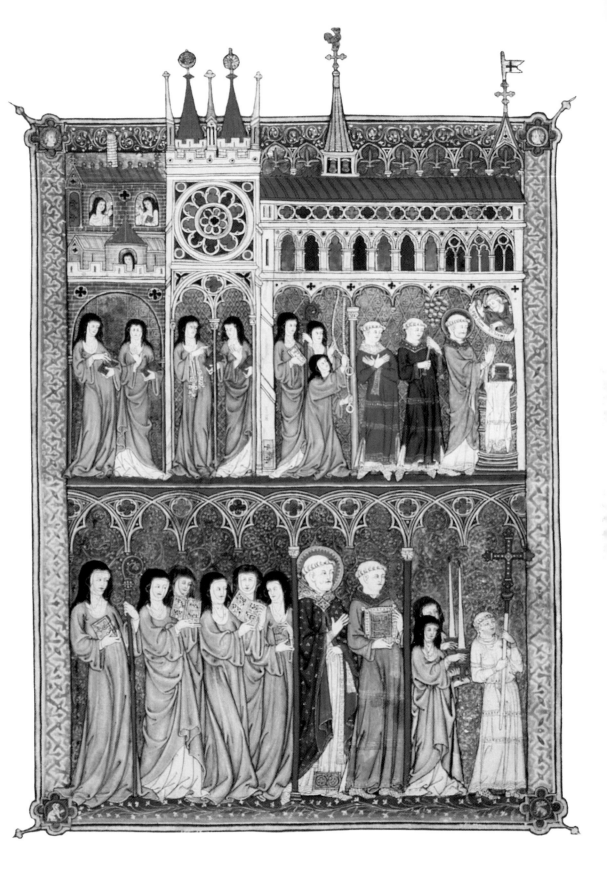

RIGHT *The elaborate ritual of the strict monastery is suggested by this illustration from a French miniature of about 1300. Nuns are shown chanting prayers and bell-ringing. They are accompanied by men because only male priests were allowed to lead the service of the mass. The nun with the keys is probably the cellarer*

Nuns and priests in procession. Ritual processions played an important part in the daily routine of organised prayer. At the rear of the procession the abbess stands with her crosier, symbol of her authority

THE POWER OF THE ABBOT

The word abbot means 'father'. For St Benedict a monastery was a family and the abbot was a stern but loving father to all his sons. The Rule demanded total obedience from monks. In return, the abbot was responsible for their souls and it was his duty to be constantly vigilant for the spiritual well-being of all members of the community:

BELOW The abbot and monks of Westminster Abbey, gathered together at the daily chapter meeting. It was in chapter that monks were obliged to confess their misdemeanours before the abbot and receive any penance or punishment

He must adapt himself to circumstances, now using severity and now persuasion, displaying the rigour of a master or the loving kindness of a father. Those of gentle disposition and good understanding should be punished by verbal admonition; but bold, hard, proud and disobedient characters should be checked by the rod and corporal punishment.

While, in theory, the power of an abbot or abbess was absolute, in practice, the leaders of monastic communities could not simply do as they pleased. If an abbot or

ABOVE The wheel of the religious life. The abbot sits at the top of the wheel overseeing the life of his monks. A wicked monk is cast down, while a virtuous monk rises upwards

RIGHT A Benedictine abbot sits in authority as one of his monks makes his vows of lifetime obedience

abbess was too autocratic monks or nuns would react badly. This appears to have happened at the abbey of Romsey in Hampshire in the thirteenth century. Archbishop John Peckham wrote an angry letter to the abbess ordering her to consult more with her nuns:

Know that thou art not mistress of the common goods, but rather the mother of thy community, according to the meaning of the word abbess. And because thou hast been wont to do too much according to the prompting of thine own will, we adjoin to thee three assistants, without whose counsel thou shalt not attempt anything pertaining to the rule of the convent.

THE THREAT OF EXILE

An abbot had considerable power over those who opposed him. They could be beaten or imprisoned and put in chains. Jocelin of Brakelond ruefully commented: 'The supreme duty of monks is to be silent and shut their eyes to the transgressions of their superiors, and sometimes we are condemned for disobedience either to imprisonment or exile.' Abbots of large Benedictine monasteries often exiled monks to a distant out-station or 'cell' of the abbey. This caused considerable resentment. Matthew Paris of St Albans said of one abbot: 'He transferred the monks of this church mercilessly from here to the cells and from cell to cell, here and there, like serfs of the lowest condition, against their will and without any fault of theirs, so that many spent all their lives in the cells, especially the remote ones, in the utmost bitterness, and died there.'

RIGHT An abbot's crosier from Hyde Abbey, Winchester, dating from the early thirteenth century. The crosier was a symbolic version of the shepherd's crook, representing the abbot's authority over his flock

SAMSON: PORTRAIT OF AN ABBOT

In the early Middle Ages many abbots were saintly characters. By contrast, by the late twelfth century the abbot of a Benedictine house was more likely to be an energetic man of business, keen to defend his legal rights. Jocelin of Brakelond gives a graphic description of a business-like abbot named Samson, who ruled the abbey of Bury St Edmunds during the years 1182–1211:

> Abbot Samson was of middle height, and almost entirely bald. His face was neither round nor long, his nose was prominent, his lips were thick, his eyes were clear as crystal and he had a penetrating glance. His eyebrows were long and were often clipped. When he became abbot he was forty-seven years old, and he had been a monk for seventeen years before that.

A great abbot was similar to other great lords. On one occasion Samson even went to war: 'He went to the siege of Windsor, at which, with certain other abbots of England, he carried arms having his own standard and leading a number of knights at great expense.' Like any other powerful noble, Samson jealously guarded his feudal rights, such as his monopoly of the local corn mills. Jocelin recounts how the abbot responded when he discovered that one tenant had built a windmill without permission:

> Herbert the Dean set up a windmill, and when the abbot heard of this he grew so hot with anger that he would scarcely eat or speak a single word. The next day he ordered his carpenters there immediately to pull everything down. The abbot said, 'By God's face, I will never eat bread till that building be thrown down.'

Samson also argued with the neighbouring monks of Ely when they established a market at Lakenheath, since he saw this as a threat to his own market at Bury St Edmunds. One night he sent 600 armed men to make a surprise attack on the rival market, telling them to seize and put in chains any market traders and customers they could find. However, the people of Lakenheath were warned of the attack and ran away. Unable to arrest anyone, Abbot Samson's army destroyed the stalls of the market traders and carried off many of their sheep and cattle.

VIOLENCE IN THE MONASTERY

The tension between the head of a monastery and a monk or nun could, very occasionally, lead to violence. When Bishop William Alnwick of Lincoln visited Catesby Priory in 1442 he was told that the prioress, Margaret Wavere, was so bad-tempered that she often used violence against her nuns. It was stated that she had attacked nuns in the convent church, tearing off their veils, dragging them by the hair and calling them beggars and harlots.

The story of how a monk was driven to murder the head of his monastery is recounted by Matthew Paris. The incident took place in the Cluniac priory of Thetford in 1248. The prior of Thetford was, according to Paris, an arrogant and immoral man. He spent much of the priory's income on his own debauched lifestyle and rarely went to church, preferring to spend his time drinking with his cronies. One day an argument broke out between the prior and a Welsh monk, who objected to the prior's decision to send him to Cluny:

> But when the prior yelled at him, this devil of a monk, in a fit of violent temper or rather seized with madness, drew a knife and disembowelled him. When the wounded prior, with the death-rattle sounding in his throat, tried by shouting to summon the monks, he could not do so because his windpipe had closed. Again the monk rushed at him and with frantic blows buried the knife right up to the hilt in his lifeless body. The king ordered the miscreant to be committed to the lowest dungeon of Norwich Castle, where he would be deprived of all light.

ABOVE *The original Benedictine ideal of the abbot as stern father is suggested in this carving of a Cistercian abbot and a kneeling monk*

BELOW *The fireplace in the abbot's parlour at Muchelney Abbey, Somerset. By the late Middle Ages most abbots lived separately from the rest of the community, and in considerable comfort*

BUILDERS AND CRAFTSMEN

While monks and nuns might have had general oversight of operations in the construction of new abbey buildings, the business of architectural design was generally carried out by laymen. The architects were usually masons by training and they were well paid. The design of medieval monastic churches was not a modern scientific enterprise. There was a large measure of trial and error in the way master masons put together these huge stone structures. Sometimes they got it badly wrong and there was a major collapse. Frequently this was the result of inadequate foundations for the building. The limitations of the design were often exposed in the towers and spires of monastic churches, and tower collapses took place at regular intervals: at Abingdon in 1091, Winchester in 1107, Gloucester in 1170, and Worcester in 1175.

The master mason was not only the architect but also had oversight of a large and varied team of workers that could include masons, carpenters, plasterers, painters, glaziers, metal-workers, tilers and unskilled labourers. Skilled masons and carpenters would travel great distances to work on a new abbey. Unskilled labour was more likely to come from the immediate area. During the construction of the Cistercian abbey of Vale Royal,

Cheshire in 1278–80, masons came from all over England including places such as Lincoln, Oxford and Salisbury.

The building season lasted from March to October. While work was in progress the workers' day started at about five o'clock in the morning, and finished at about seven o'clock at night. As long as the work lasted the pay was relatively good. At the end of October, however, building stopped, and any unfinished work was covered with straw or bracken to prevent frost damage. In the winter the majority of workers were laid off. Only a small number of the more skilled masons would be retained to work on fine details in the mason's shelter or lodge.

Some work also took place at the quarry. Transporting stone was very expensive and costs were cut by sending templates to the quarry so that masons could shape the stone there first.

ABOVE *A medieval mason at work. Masons were the most important members of the teams of builders responsible for new monastic buildings. The architect was usually a master mason*

LEFT *An angel assists Benedictine monks to build an abbey in a twelfth-century illustration from Durham Cathedral Priory. In reality, monks and nuns were rarely involved in the manual labour of building after the early Middle Ages*

ABOVE *Builders at work in about 1240. This was drawn by Matthew Paris of St Albans. In his writings he chronicled the almost constant building work that took place at his abbey*

RIGHT *Plumbers were active on monastic building sites. These medieval taps come from Lewes Priory, Waltham Abbey and Fountains Abbey*

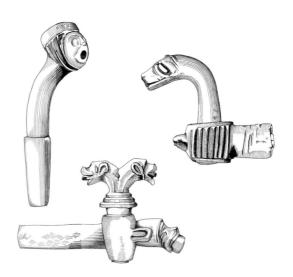

BELOW *An imaginative reconstruction of building work at Tintern Abbey in Wales in the late thirteenth century. Tintern was one of the first Cistercian houses in Britain. The early Cistercians prided themselves on the simplicity of their churches and insisted on a plainer architectural style than that of the Benedictines at the same period. The first church at Tintern, built in the twelfth century, was large but plain. Eventually the Cistercians relaxed their opposition to elaborate and ornate buildings and Tintern was completely rebuilt after 1269 in a much grander style*

The plain church and monastic buildings of the twelfth century. The plan of these early Cistercian abbeys was almost identical, whether the abbey was in Wales, Yorkshire or France

ABOVE *A sketch plan of the original, simple design of the Cistercian abbey at Tintern*

The east end of the new abbey church. In 1269 the builders began to create a new church without immediately demolishing the old one. This was because the building campaign would last for many years and it was necessary to minimise the disruption to the abbey's religious services. It was not until 1288 that monks were able to move from the old church to the choir of the new one, and many more years before the whole building was complete

The west end of the new abbey church. The old church eventually had to be pulled down before the whole of the new design could be completed. While the work was carried out the site would have been thronging with craftsmen and labourers. This must have interfered with the peace and tranquillity prescribed for the Cistercian way of life

19

ARTISTIC EXCELLENCE

BELOW *The Syon Cope, one of the finest surviving church vestments of the Middle Ages. It was the property of Syon, a distinguished nunnery near London. It is not known where the cope was made, but it dates from about 1300, before Syon was founded. It is an example of 'opus anglicanum', a style of embroidery that was distinctively English*

Although monks were rarely responsible for the design of their beautiful church buildings, they did create almost all the great illuminated manuscripts produced before 1200. This tradition went back to the earliest days of English monasticism. The Lindisfarne Gospels were created around 700 and are as fine as anything produced in the rest of Europe at the time. The artist responsible for them was probably Eadfrith, the bishop and abbot of Lindisfarne.

leading Norman abbots were too busy with their administrative duties to spend time personally on illumination, and most of the finest illuminators of the twelfth century were anonymous choir monks. There was a final great flowering of the monastic illuminator's art in the years 1220–70.

Illumination was organised by the cantor or precentor, the monk responsible for the chanting in the abbey church. In theory, the main purpose of illuminated manuscripts was to provide service books for use in church. Most manuscripts were produced in the cloister, where the alley nearest to the church was usually designated the 'scriptorium', or place for work on calligraphy and illumination.

At Gloucester Cathedral, a former Benedictine monastery, the study cubicles or carrells can still be seen in the cloister. In the early Middle Ages the cloister was not usually glazed and monks complained that in winter work on manuscripts was sometimes impossible.

During the monastic revival of the tenth century English monks won a reputation for the quality of their craftwork. The greatest abbots of late Saxon times were themselves often highly talented artists. St Dunstan was not only a great monastic leader but was also a talented illuminator, musician and metal-worker. After the Norman Conquest individual monks continued to excel as craftsmen. In the early twelfth century, Hugh, the sacrist of Bury St Edmunds, personally cast the bronze doors and bells of the church. Despite individual examples such as Hugh, however, leading Norman monks placed much less emphasis on these practical skills. After the Conquest fine metalwork was more likely to be the handiwork of paid lay craftsmen.

For many English nuns the main form of artistic work was the embroidery of vestments and altar decorations. English needlework, known as 'opus anglicanum', was renowned throughout Europe, especially in the late thirteenth and early fourteenth centuries. Much of this fine embroidery was exported.

In the age of Bede (see p.30) it was common for distinguished abbots to find the time to produce illuminated manuscripts. Illumination came to a stop as a result of the Viking attacks but was revived after 940 by St Dunstan and his follower Aethelwold. In the tenth century the two monasteries of Winchester became centres of excellence in illumination. The greatest product of the Winchester school was the Benedictional of St Aethelwold of about 980.

The Norman Conquest again disrupted the production of illuminated manuscripts for a time. Illumination of quality recommenced in the twelfth century and reached an artistic peak in the years 1140–80, during which English illumination was, once again, as fine as any in Europe. Unlike the Anglo-Saxons, the

ABOVE *A wall painting of the patron saint from the refectory of Horsham St Faith Priory, Norfolk, dating from the thirteenth century. Many of the walls of medieval monasteries were decorated with murals but most were destroyed at the time of the Reformation*

ABOVE *A thimble from Thornholme Priory, Yorkshire. Several thimbles were found near the choir stalls, suggesting that mending took place during services!*

ABOVE *A pharmaceutical mortar from St Mary's Abbey, York. It was made by a craftsman-monk, and is inscribed 'Brother William of Towthorpe made me 1308'*

ABOVE *This small lead ink pot from Battle Abbey in Sussex contained traces of bright red ink*

ABOVE *A bone parchment 'pricker' from Battle Abbey. This would have been used to prick holes at the end of each line of text to ensure it aligned correctly*

Between the collapse of Roman power in the fifth century and the emergence of the universities in the mid-twelfth century, monasteries were the only centres of higher education and learning in England. It was in monasteries that the learning of classical antiquity was kept alive. Before 1150 literature and scholarship were completely dominated by the work of Benedictine monks. These scholar-monks particularly specialised in the writing of history. The three greatest English historians of the Middle Ages were monks: Bede, William of Malmesbury and Matthew Paris.

ancient Rome. Knowledge of Greek was rare, but monks read pagan Latin authors such as Horace, Virgil and Ovid.

SCHOLARSHIP AMONG NUNS

In Anglo-Saxon times English nuns were renowned for their scholarship. An eighth-century English nun named Lioba, for example, composed poetry in Latin; later in her career she went to Germany to help St Boniface and

BELOW *A pioneering map of Britain, drawn by Matthew Paris in about 1250. His own abbey of St Albans is shown to the north of London. Paris himself was surprisingly well travelled for a monk; in 1248, for example, he visited Norway in order to reorganise an abbey near Trondheim*

ABOVE *The Virgin and child by Matthew Paris, about 1250. Below the main image is a self-portrait of the artist. Paris was an extremely gifted man who excelled in historical writing and a range of artistic activities*

Medieval books were, of course, precious hand-written objects. A great abbey might have had about 600 books in the late twelfth century. A small monastery would probably have had fewer than 100. In addition to religious texts, library catalogues also included books on music, history, medicine and the prose and poetry of

finally became abbess of Bischofheim. Her biographer recounts how 'she was so bent on reading that she never laid aside her book except to pray or to strengthen her slight frame with food and sleep. From childhood upwards she had studied grammar and the other liberal arts.'

This level of female education did not last throughout the medieval period. The nuns of the later Middle Ages in England were not noted for their scholarship. While some nuns on the Continent were distinguished writers, in England there is no evidence after the Conquest of women copying manuscripts or writing chronicles. Knowledge of Latin, an important aspect of education, was

ABOVE *Reconstruction drawing of a pair of medieval spectacles based on a fragment found at Battle Abbey. In 1286 the Franciscan friar Roger Bacon made the earliest known reference to the use of lenses for reading*

rare amongst nuns by the fourteenth century. The Rule of St Benedict was translated into English but those who could not read Latin spent many hours singing Latin prayers in choir without knowing what they meant.

MONKS AND MEDICINE

There was a strong tradition of medical knowledge in many monasteries. William the Conqueror's own doctor was Baldwin, abbot of Bury St Edmunds. Faricius, abbot of Abingdon, was physician to Henry I and his wife, Matilda. The abbey at Abingdon gained several valuable gifts from

university-trained laymen and monks in medical practice became much less common.

The study of urine was one of the main techniques used by doctors in the Middle Ages. They followed the teachings of the Romans who believed that the colour of urine was a key indicator of health. The chronicler Matthew Paris told how the twelfth-century Abbot John of St Albans examined his own urine to work out how long he had left to live:

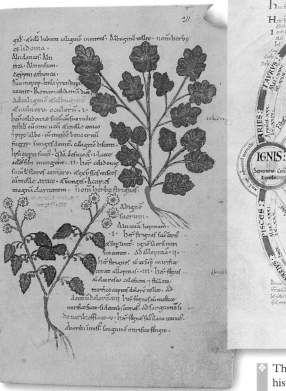

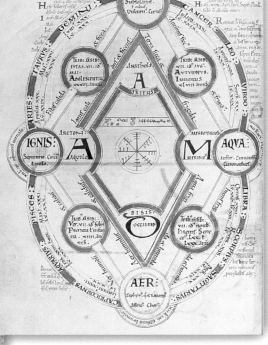

Faricius's large circle of wealthy patients. Warin, the abbot of St Albans in the late twelfth century, had studied medicine at the famous medical school at Salerno, in southern Italy.

Monastic doctors could make large sums of money for their abbeys. The chronicle of Evesham Abbey records that in about the year 1200 the cost of the abbey's new tower was largely met by the fees of the monk-physician, Thomas of Northwick. Some people criticised the practice of medicine by monks on the grounds that it was mercenary and likely to lead to improper contact with women. Church councils repeatedly urged monks not to work as doctors. In the later Middle Ages leading doctors tended to be

The next day he carefully examined his urine, to see what it portended, for he was an excellent physician, and also an incomparable judge of urine. Although he inspected it diligently he was unable, because the keenness of his eyesight had been in a large measure blunted, to observe to his liking the subtle and secret signs of death, which he knew. So he said to one of our monks, Master William the Physician, 'What do you see here, brother?' He indicated what he saw, and the abbot said, 'Ah! Praise be to God! He has allowed me three more days for penance; but after the three days I shall die.' Those who heard this believed it, for he was most experienced in the art of medicine and had often infallibly foretold similar things concerning others in such circumstances. *(Matthew Paris)*

A SAINTLY MONK

ABOVE *St Bernard writing and teaching. When Bernard met Aelred he ordered him to write a book explaining the idea of charitable love*

BELOW *King David of Scotland. Aelred sacrificed a glittering career at the Scottish court to pursue his monastic vocation*

For most medieval monks and nuns we lack detailed records that would enable us to see them as complete, rounded personalities. One important exception to this is the figure of Aelred, Abbot of Rievaulx Abbey in Yorkshire. We know a considerable amount about Aelred both from his own writings and those of a disciple, Walter Daniel, who wrote a detailed biography. Aelred was born in about 1110 and, unlike many of his monastic contemporaries, his family was Anglo-Saxon rather than Norman. His father was a married priest from Hexham in Northumberland (celibacy was not enforced throughout the Catholic Church until later). As a monk Aelred looked back to his childhood and gave an attractive picture of the importance he had then attached to friendship:

> When I was still a boy at school, the friendship of those around me was my greatest joy, and I gave myself up wholly to my affection for my friends, so that to love and be loved seemed the most delightful thing in the world, and nothing else seemed of any profit at all.

He was educated with members of the Scottish royal family and as a young man he joined the court of David, king of Scotland. Aelred did well and was promoted to the powerful post of steward to the king. Despite this prestigious job, Aelred felt dissatisfied with life. In 1134 he was sent by King David on a mission south to visit the archbishop of York. He heard from a friend about the saintly Cistercian monks who had established themselves at Rievaulx, in the valley of the River Rye, two years earlier. Having completed his business in York, Aelred visited Rievaulx and spent a day at the abbey. He stayed the night at the nearby castle of Helmsley. The next day, as he was setting out for Scotland, Aelred rode along the ridge of a hill and looked down on Rievaulx. He was overwhelmed by a desire to join the community and he changed course then and there, presenting himself for admission at the doors of the abbey.

FRIENDSHIP IN THE CLOISTER

The preoccupation with love and friendship which Aelred showed as a child continued in the cloister. In his writings he tells of the intense spiritual relationships he had with other monks at Rievaulx. Of one close companion, Simon, who died young, he wrote, 'I chose him as friend and companion in the joys of the cloister and the delights of the spirit which I was then tasting for the first time. I asked nothing, I gave nothing but affection and the loving judgement which affection gave.'

PROMOTION

Aelred rapidly became one of the leading members of the community at Rievaulx. He was appointed novice-master, and soon afterwards he became the founding abbot of Revesby Abbey in Lincolnshire. In 1147, at the age of thirty-seven, he was returned to Rievaulx as abbot. Even before his promotion Aelred was a figure of some importance in the Cistercian world. In 1142 he was sent to Rome as the abbot's representative. This may have been the first occasion on which he met Bernard of Clairvaux as he passed through France. Bernard was impressed by Aelred and ordered him to write a book on the subject of charitable love.

CENTRE LEFT *Two young Cistercians studying together. Aelred attached great importance to friendship*

BELOW *The cloisters at Fontenay in Burgundy give a good impression of the architecture of Rievaulx in Aelred's time*

ABOVE *The travels of Aelred*

BELOW *Rievaulx Abbey today. Aelred decided to join when he looked down on the abbey from above*

AN ENERGETIC ABBOT

In his later years Aelred wrote extensively on a wide range of issues, including both historical and religious works. His writings are all the more remarkable because as abbot of Rievaulx his responsibilities were burdensome. Like all other Cistercian abbots Aelred visited Cîteaux every September for the general chapter meeting. In addition, he was required once a year to attend discussions at Clairvaux, the mother-house of Rievaulx. He was also obliged to inspect annually the five 'daughter houses' of the abbey: Woburn, Revesby and Rufford in England and Melrose and Dundrennan in Scotland. Aelred played a prominent part in the political world of the time and corresponded with English, Scottish and French royalty.

Despite the range of demands on his time, Aelred was anxious not to neglect Rievaulx. He was a talented administrator as well as a man of great holiness. The last ten years of his life were marred by severe illness but despite this he continued to inspire the rest of the community. Walter Daniel tells how crowds of monks would come to visit him when he was confined to bed through illness, 'some sitting on his very bed as little children might on that of their mother'. Aelred died in 1167, at Rievaulx, surrounded by his monks.

ABOVE *Aelred was passionately devoted to Christ and his mother, the Blessed Virgin*

ABOVE *The young Aelred portrayed in a French Cistercian manuscript. He inspired intense love among his fellow monks*

RIGHT *The early thirteenth-century presbytery at Rievaulx, a fine setting for the high altar and St Aelred's shrine. Aelred himself would almost certainly have disapproved of the elaborate architecture that developed around his shrine*

THE ORIGINS OF MONASTIC LIFE

Monasticism was at its height in the Middle Ages.
But how did it arrive and become established in Britain?
The first monks lived in the Middle East in the final years of the
Roman Empire. Their ideals - modified over time - were brought to
Britain by successive waves of invaders. Celts, Saxons, Vikings
and Normans all played a part in the evolution of monastic life.

THE FIRST MONKS

ABOVE *St Antony was one of the founders of Christian monasticism. Antony and his followers sought to escape from a sinful world and find God through a life of prayer in the Egyptian desert. Monks and nuns in subsequent centuries often tried to emulate the first 'desert fathers' by establishing themselves in wild, deserted places*

BELOW *Later in the Middle Ages the Camoldolese monks in Italy tried to imitate the lives of the hermits of the Egyptian desert*

In about the year 300 an Egyptian Christian named Antony decided to leave his village in order to devote himself entirely to prayer, living as a hermit in the desert. Others were impressed by his lifestyle and went to live near him. Within a few years these people were described as 'monks', from a Greek word meaning 'single' or 'solitary'. Although Antony sought to live alone, some of these pioneering monks soon began to explore the idea of living a life of prayer together in a community. In about 320 Pachomius, another Egyptian, began to organise groups of followers into permanent communities or monasteries. From these earliest times women, as well as men, were attracted to the monastic ideal. Together with his sister Mary, Pachomius founded two monasteries for women.

The monks of the Egyptian desert sought to live a life of Christian perfection. Since sex was regarded as sinful, they pledged themselves to a life of celibacy. They gave away all their worldly goods and lived in complete poverty. They tried to cut themselves off completely from their family and former friends. The monastic life was one of renunciation – giving up all the pleasures of ordinary life in order to come closer to God through constant prayer.

EXTREME SELF-DENIAL

Renunciation was taken by some monks to extremes. An Egyptian monk, Pior, refused to see any member of his family for fifty years. When a bishop finally ordered him to meet his sister he agreed only on condition that he kept his eyes closed throughout the interview!

A monastic writer of the fifth century described approvingly how another of the first monks also refused to communicate with his family. After fifteen years he finally received a large package of letters.

> 'What thoughts,' said he, 'will the reading of these suggest to me? They will incite me to senseless joy or useless sadness.' So he threw the whole packet into the fire, all tied up just as he had received it. *(Cassian)*

BELOW *Early monasticism in the eastern Mediterranean*

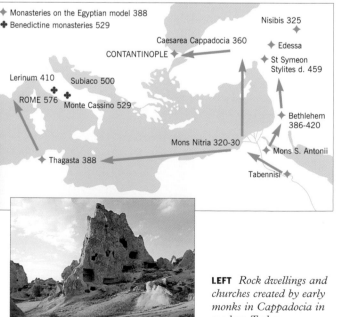

✦ Monasteries on the Egyptian model 388
✚ Benedictine monasteries 529

Nisibis 325
Caesarea Cappadocia 360
✦ Edessa
CONTANTINOPLE
✦ St Symeon Stylites d. 459
Lerinum 410   Subiaco 500
✚   ✚
ROME 576   Monte Cassino 529
✦ Bethlehem 386-420
Mons Nitria 320-30
✦ Thagasta 388
✦ Mons S. Antonii
Tabennisi ✦

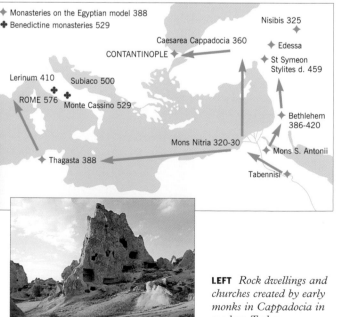

LEFT *Rock dwellings and churches created by early monks in Cappadocia in modern Turkey*

The monastic life gradually spread throughout the Christian world. As it did so some monks continued to subject themselves to extraordinary suffering. Many of the most extreme examples of monastic self-denial came from Syria. In the early fifth century Symeon the Stylite ('pillar-dweller') won many admirers by spending over thirty years chained to the top of a high pillar. Crowds gathered to watch and hear him speak. Symeon often stood all night with his arms outstretched in prayer.

Not all monks admired this excessively solitary lifestyle. The idea of a more moderate community life was developed in Caesarea in modern Turkey by St Basil in the mid-fourth century. After his death in 379 Basil's ideas were written down as a rule for monastic life. The Rule of St Basil was very influential and has remained the guiding set of principles for monks in the Eastern Orthodox Church up to the present day.

SAINTS BASIL AND BENEDICT

In his Rule St Basil stated clearly that the life of a hermit was not desirable because it was self-centred and indulgent; monks needed to live together if they were to follow Christ's teaching about how we should serve other people:

> The solitary life has one aim, the service of the needs of the individual. But this is plainly in conflict with the law of love. Whose feet then wilt thou wash? Whom wilt thou care for? (The Rule of St Basil)

The more moderate, communal monasticism of St Basil was paralleled in western Europe by the work of St Benedict, an Italian monk of the early sixth century. Like St Basil he deliberately rejected the extreme aspects of some forms of early monasticism. Benedict began his career as a solitary hermit but he attracted followers and subsequently organised them into communities at Monte Cassino and Subiaco. Like Basil, Benedict wrote a Rule in order to instruct his monks how they should live their lives. This written guidance had a very substantial impact on medieval monasticism in western Europe; in England between 700 and 1100 AD Benedictine monks and nuns virtually monopolised monastic life.

Though a brief document, the Rule manages to set out with great clarity how the daily life of a monastery should be organised. Precise details are given on such matters as how new recruits should be welcomed and recalcitrant monks punished. Monks are instructed to divide their time between prayer and work. The communal recital of the Book of Psalms from the Old Testament is the central feature of daily worship. To modern readers the Rule may seem strict but Benedict himself claimed that he was establishing a way of serving God 'in which nothing harsh or burdensome will be ordained'. The Rule stressed the paramount importance of obedience: the monk must submit himself totally to the authority of the abbot. Benedict also required his followers to practise complete personal poverty. Through obedience and poverty the monk should seek to destroy selfish inclinations and achieve closer union with God.

ABOVE *A fourth-century sculpture of Christ washing the feet of St Peter. This image was popular among the first monks because it symbolised the humility of Christ. Throughout the history of monasticism committed monks and nuns have tried to imitate Christ and have emphasised the importance of humility and self-denial*

CENTRE RIGHT *A copy of the Rule of St Benedict, of about 1100. The Rule laid down how a monastery should be organised and how its members should conduct their life of work and formal worship. Benedict rejected the excesses of some early monks and described a more moderate, communal lifestyle. The Rule recognised that there would be unworthy and recalcitrant monks and described how they should be disciplined*

ABOVE *St Benedict in an eleventh-century illustration from Canterbury Cathedral Priory. For much of the Middle Ages the teachings of Benedict had a dominant influence on monasticism in western Europe. The inscription on the saint's halo refers to him as the father of monks*

MISSIONARIES COME TO BRITAIN

Monks played a central part in the conversion of Anglo-Saxon England to Christianity. They came from two quite distinct traditions: the Celtic and the Italian.

CELTIC MISSIONARIES
In the early fifth century monasteries began to be established in Ireland by monks from Gaul (modern France). An influential figure at this time was St Patrick, a Gaul whose first contact with Ireland was when, as a young

ABOVE *There was a strong tradition of travel and missionary work among early Irish monks. Here St Brendan and his companions encounter perils at sea*

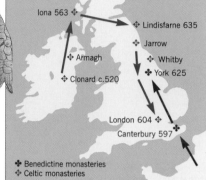

ABOVE RIGHT *The two-pronged conversion of the English: Italian monks began missionary work in Kent; Celtic monks took the Christian message to Northumbria*

BELOW *An eighth-century casket containing a relic of St Columba, the founder of Iona. Columba was a leading figure in Celtic monasticism. Monks from Iona led the missionary effort to convert the northern Anglo-Saxons*

man, he was kidnapped and taken there as a slave. He escaped, but in the middle years of the fifth century he returned to Ireland as a preacher.

Whereas the Celtic population of the British Isles was Christian, the Anglo-Saxons who settled there in the fifth and sixth centuries were heathens. The monks of Ireland were instrumental in bringing Christianity to northern Britain. Much missionary activity was carried out by Columba, an Irish monk who in 563 founded a monastery on Iona, a small Scottish island near Mull.

ST AUGUSTINE
Later in the sixth century, in Italy, a Benedictine monk named Gregory became Pope. According to tradition, Gregory saw a group of Anglo-Saxon slaves for sale in the marketplace in Rome and was struck by their appearance. When he was told that the slaves were heathen Angles, he commented: 'That is appropriate, for they have angelic faces'. In 596 Gregory launched a missionary campaign to win the English over to Christianity. His team of

monks was headed by Augustine, prior of the abbey of St Andrew in Rome.

Augustine reached England in 597, the same year in which Columba died. At this time Anglo-Saxon England was divided into a number of kingdoms, and Gregory had instructed Augustine and his monks to convert the royal families, calculating that their people would quickly follow suit. The nearest kingdom was that of Kent, whose king, Ethelbert, was one of the most powerful of the English rulers. His wife was a Frankish princess and already a Christian. Anticipating a friendly reception, Augustine decided to make his landing in Kent. His strategy proved successful, and Augustine and his monks made their headquarters at Canterbury, which has been the centre of English Christianity ever since.

Augustine's task was not to be easily accomplished, however. He had assumed that the Celtic monks would accept him as the primate, or leading churchman of all Britain, but on two separate occasions they refused to recognise his authority. Augustine died in 604, having achieved much in his lifetime. However, the tension between the Celtic and the Benedictine monks continued after his death.

ABOVE *A medieval depiction of the shrine of St Augustine at St Augustine's Abbey, Canterbury. The shrine incorporated a number of books which Augustine was said to have brought from Rome*

BELOW *A fifteenth-century stained-glass depiction of St Augustine*

ABOVE *St Augustine's Abbey, Canterbury. The Italian missionary Augustine established this monastic community to the east of the town of Canterbury, the capital of Kent. The abbey was dedicated to the memory of Augustine in the tenth century*

TWO TRADITIONS

Celtic monks, isolated from Rome, had developed a number of different traditions from the Benedictine monks of Italy, such as Augustine. The abbot of a Celtic monastery was not only in charge of his monks, but also held authority over the whole Church in the area. Even bishops were subordinate to the local abbot. Another difference was that monks did not spend all their time in the monastery; they provided pastoral care to lay people and frequently undertook missionary journeys.

Celtic monks were involved in the conversion of the powerful northern kingdom of Northumbria. In 635 the Northumbrian king Oswald decided to become a Christian and invited the monks of Iona to send him a bishop. Bishop Aidan established a monastery on the tidal island of Lindisfarne, run on similar lines to Iona:

ABOVE *A reconstruction illustration of St Cuthbert's hermitage on the island of Inner Farne, Northumberland, in the late seventh century. The Celtic tradition encouraged the most committed monks, such as the saintly Cuthbert, to lead the solitary life of a hermit*

The king always listened humbly and readily to Aidan's advice and diligently set himself to establish and extend the Church of Christ throughout his kingdom. Henceforward many Scots arrived day by day in Britain and proclaimed the word of God with great devotion in all the provinces under Oswald's rule. Most of those who came to preach were monks.
(Bede, 'A History of the English Church and People')

In many areas there was resistance to the new ideas, and it was seventy years before every English kingdom was converted. Christianity and monasticism went hand in hand. As the new religion gained ground, so monasteries were gradually established in every part of the country.

Arguments between the Irish-Celtic and Roman-Benedictine monks continued during the seventh century.

Disagreements centred on different methods of calculating the date of Easter. The disputes finally came to a head in the early 660s. Oswy, the king of Northumbria, had been taught to follow the ways of the Celtic monks of Lindisfarne whereas his wife, Eanfled, who came from Kent, was used to the

Roman traditions. In 664 Oswy convened a conference or synod at the abbey of Whitby to resolve the differences between Celtic and Benedictine monks. Leading churchmen from both sides came to argue their case, and at last Oswy ruled that the Roman-Benedictine arguments were superior. Since he was the most powerful king in England, his decision to back the Roman party was crucial. Roman monasticism had triumphed over Celtic monasticism. The abbot of Lindisfarne accepted defeat and left England taking many of his Celtic monks with him. After Whitby, English monks organised themselves on similar lines to the monasteries of Gaul and Italy.

ABOVE *An artist's impression of the abbey church on Lindisfarne, about 650. The church was built in the Irish style, of oak and thatch. The community at Lindisfarne was protected by the royal family of Northumbria. The lifestyle of these early Northumbrian monks was austere and demanding*

THE AGE OF BEDE

Monasticism had a particularly strong impact on the northern kingdom of Northumbria. The early monasteries were often extremely cosmopolitan. One Northumbrian abbot, named Benedict Biscop, made frequent visits to Gaul and Italy, returning with books, vestments, paintings and other works of art; these encouraged the production of fine religious art in English monasteries. Biscop also brought stone masons and glaziers from Gaul and encouraged the change from timber to stone church buildings. He set up new monasteries at Monkwearmouth and Jarrow. In 680 the Pope agreed to send John, the Benedictine choirmaster of St Peter's in Rome, to instruct the monks of the monastery of Monkwearmouth and other English abbeys. This distinguished visitor ensured that the English monks chanted their prayers in the same style as the Benedictines of Italy.

There was a great intellectual vitality about these early English monasteries. The monks and nuns, themselves highly educated, brought a new level of education to the English people. Manuscript books of the highest quality were produced. The Lindisfarne Gospels, produced in about 700 and now in the British Museum, are a particularly fine example of the illumination and calligraphy of the early monks.

ABOVE *A leaded brass censer which probably belonged to the seventh-century abbey at Glastonbury, Somerset. The censer was made many miles away, somewhere in the Byzantine Empire, and provides evidence of the links that existed between the first English monasteries and the wider world*

A NEW RECRUIT

Around the year 680 a talented young boy named Bede joined the community at Jarrow. He was to become a prolific and famous writer, and his work tells us much about life in the earliest English monasteries.

Bede's own life was one dedicated to prayer and study. The daily round at Jarrow centred on the church and the chanted prayers and psalms that were sung at regular intervals throughout the night and day. Work took a variety of forms: study, the illumination of manuscripts, farming, care of guests and domestic tasks around the abbey.

DELIGHT IN STUDY

The work of Bede is generally regarded as the finest historical writing, not only of the Anglo-Saxon period, but of the whole of the Middle Ages. His most famous work, *A History of the English Church and People*, tells the story of the Anglo-Saxons from their arrival in Britain to Bede's own time. At the end, Bede gives a brief autobiographical sketch:

> I was born on the lands of this monastery, and on reaching seven years of age, I was entrusted by my family first to the most reverend Abbot Benedict and later to Abbot Ceolfrid for my education. I have spent all the remainder of my life in this monastery and devoted myself entirely to the study of the Scriptures. And while I have observed the regular discipline and sung the choir offices daily in church, my chief delight has always been in study, teaching and writing.

Although the age of Bede was generally a time of high achievement, not all monks and nuns lived up to the highest standards. Bede told of a monk he knew who was a good craftsman but not at all suited to monastic life:

> He was a skilled worker in metal. But he was much addicted to drunkenness and the other pleasures of a loose life, and used to remain in his workshop day and night rather than enter the church to sing and pray.

ABOVE *A reconstruction illustration of the monastery at Jarrow in its early days. Together with its sister house in Monkwearmouth, Jarrow was a centre of great learning and culture. Bede spent almost all his life as a monk at this abbey*

THE LIFE OF ST CUTHBERT

While Bede's own life was spent in a community, some monks preferred the life of a hermit; indeed Bede admired the self-discipline of those who chose the solitary spiritual life. It was believed that such hermits were engaged in a daily battle with the forces of evil, and that only the holiest were capable of this way of life. One of Bede's heroes was the monk, Cuthbert. After training in the Scottish abbey of Melrose Cuthbert became prior of Lindisfarne. Later, however, he decided to pursue the life of a hermit and left the community to live on the nearby island of Inner Farne:

> Now the island had no water, corn, or trees, and being the haunt of evil spirits was very ill-suited to human habitation. But when the man of God came, he ordered the evil spirits to withdraw, and the island became quite habitable. (Bede)

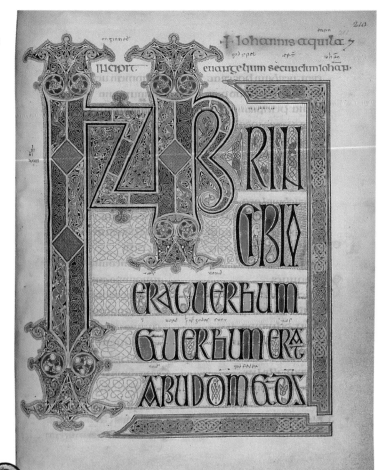

ABOVE *The first page of St John's Gospel, from the Lindisfarne Gospels. This beautiful illuminated manuscript was produced at the monastery of Lindisfarne in about 700, shortly after the discovery of Cuthbert's undecayed body. The artist was a monk named Eadfrith who became bishop of Lindisfarne in about 698*

ABOVE
One of the treasures of Durham Cathedral is this seventh-century gold cross, which was probably once worn by Cuthbert

The brothers from Lindisfarne helped Cuthbert to dig a well, and he grew barley for food. He spent many years in silence and meditation on the island, but in 685 he was forced to leave his hermitage to become bishop of Lindisfarne. After two energetic years as bishop Cuthbert returned to Inner Farne to die. Soon after his death he came to be viewed as a saint and became a focus for prayer. Bede recounts how the monks of Lindisfarne dug up his body in 698 and describes their astonishment on discovering that the body had not decayed. This was seen as proof of Cuthbert's sanctity and Lindisfarne subsequently became a centre of pilgrimage as people came to pray at his shrine.

ABOVE LEFT *A twelfth-century drawing of the discovery of Cuthbert's undecayed body in 698, eleven years after his death. Cuthbert's fame spread rapidly after this miracle and many pilgrims made their way to his shrine*

RIGHT *Bede deeply admired the saintly life of Cuthbert. This twelfth-century picture of the saint comes from a copy of a biography of Cuthbert by Bede*

31

SAXON WHITBY

In his work Bede describes several distinguished nuns. The early Church in England differed from that of the later Middle Ages in that it allowed women to play a leading part. The monastic life was particularly attractive to female members of the Anglo-Saxon royal and noble families. The most notable of these was the famous abbess of Whitby, named Hilda, who died in 680. Hilda was born in about 614 and was related to the royal family of Northumbria. At the age of thirty-three she renounced the life of a noblewoman and decided to become a nun. Her first intention was to go to Gaul, where her sister was already living as a nun. However, St Aidan of Lindisfarne persuaded her to remain in England and she became the abbess of a convent in Hartlepool. Her work at Hartlepool was greatly admired and, after several years, she was asked in 657 to found a new monastery at Whitby.

Bede was full of praise for Whitby Abbey at the time of Hilda:

ABOVE *Hilda as depicted on late medieval stained glass from Christ Church, Oxford. The memory of Hilda as a person of exceptional holiness was kept alive throughout the Middle Ages*

LEFT *Part of the tomb of St Elfleda, the third abbess of Whitby, found in excavations. Like Hilda, Elfleda was a member of the royal family of Northumbria. As a girl she joined Hilda's community at Hartlepool. She moved with her to Whitby and ultimately became abbess. She was a close friend of St Cuthbert*

ABOVE *A thirteenth-century seal from Hartlepool showing St Hilda. Hilda was abbess of Hartlepool before she moved to Whitby*

> After the example of the primitive Church, no one there was rich, no one was needy, for everything was held in common, and nothing was considered to be anyone's personal property. So great was her prudence that not only ordinary folk, but kings and princes used to come and ask for her advice in their difficulties.

The community at Whitby was a mixed one of men and women, the monks and nuns living in separate sections of the monastery. Such double monasteries were not unusual at the time and were based on monasteries found in Gaul. Further double monasteries ruled by women were later established, such as Ely in 673. Whitby, under Hilda, was a great centre of scholarship and several of the monks of her monastery went on to become bishops.

A ROYAL MONASTERY

Hilda suffered a painful illness for over six years before her death in 680. Bede wrote approvingly of her patience during this long illness, during which

ABOVE *The ruins of Whitby Abbey today. None of the existing remains date back to the time of Hilda. The original abbey was destroyed in a Viking attack in about 867 but the abbey was re-founded after the Norman Conquest*

she continued her life of prayer and religious instruction. After her death several of her nuns began to see visions and to claim that Hilda was responsible for miracles. Bede's account of these visions gives us a glimpse into the world of the early nuns:

> One sister, who loved her dearly, saw her soul ascend to heaven in the company of angels. At this time the nun was with other handmaids of Christ in a remote part of the monastery, where novices were admitted to test their vocation until they were fully instructed and admitted to membership of the community.

Whitby had strong associations with the royal family of Northumbria. Following Hilda's death, the next abbess was Enfleda, the widowed former queen of Northumbria. She in turn was succeeded by her own daughter, Elfleda. Like Hilda, both Enfleda and Elfleda had reputations for holiness. It appears that the kings of Northumbria saw Whitby as their family monastery and a place for their own burial.

The double monasteries such as Whitby were swept away following the Viking attacks (see p.34). Whitby itself was abandoned in 867. The abbey fell into ruins and these ruins were later demolished by monks of the Norman period. Nothing now survives above ground of Hilda's abbey. Fragmentary archaeological evidence suggests that the monasteries of Hilda's time had a very different layout to that of later medieval monasteries. Excavations in the 1920s examined what was probably the domestic area for the nuns, revealing that the earliest buildings were of timber. There appear to have been a number of individual cells, each with a living room and a separate bedroom. The living rooms each had a hearth for a fire and there was a latrine in the bedroom. The archaeological finds also shed some light on the daily lives of the nuns. In one room 'styli' (pointed instruments used for writing) were found, as well as pins, needles and a quern for grinding corn. In other rooms there were loom-weights, an indication that the sisters spent some of their time weaving cloth.

CAEDMON, THE POET OF WHITBY

One of the most distinguished monks of Whitby was the poet, Caedmon. He came from a humble background and was working as a farm labourer at Whitby when he was inspired in a dream to start composing sacred songs in English. He was brought before Abbess Hilda and showed her his compositions. She was convinced of his ability and encouraged him to join the abbey; here Caedmon was able to develop his gift for religious poetry and song:

> He sang of the creation of the world, the origin of the human race, and the whole story of Genesis. He sang of Israel's exodus from Egypt, the entry into the Promised Land, and many other events of scriptural history. He sang of the Lord's Incarnation, Passion, Resurrection, and Ascension into heaven, the coming of the Holy Spirit, and the teaching of the Apostles. He also made many poems on the terrors of the Last Judgement, the horrible pains of Hell, and the joys of the Kingdom of Heaven. *(Bede)*

NORMAN WHITBY

After the Norman Conquest, monks from Evesham re-established several of the Northumbrian monasteries, including Whitby. The revived monastery at Whitby was a very different place from Hilda's abbey: it was an all-male institution. While St Hilda continued to be venerated for her holiness, no women in the later Middle Ages had the power and influence of the great abbess of Whitby.

ABOVE *An Anglo-Saxon silver cross excavated at Whitby Abbey in the 1920s*

BELOW *An illustration from an eleventh-century manuscript of Caedmon's poems. He wrote in English rather than Latin, and always chose religious themes. This picture of Adam and Eve accompanies a poem on the subject*

BELOW *Hilda and her nuns saw themselves as handmaids of Christ. Anglo-Saxon devotion to Christ is reflected in this cross-shaft which probably shows Christ on the Day of Judgement*

THE VIKING ONSLAUGHT

In June 793 Viking raiders attacked Lindisfarne, killing some of the monks and robbing the treasure of the monastery. This was the start of a long period of such raids on the monasteries of the British Isles. Far away at the court of the great Frankish ruler Charlemagne, an English priest named Alcuin wrote to express his dismay at the news from Northumbria:

◆ It is nearly 350 years that we and our fathers have inhabited this most lovely land, and never before has such terror appeared in Britain as we have now suffered from a pagan race, nor was it thought that such an inroad from the sea could be made. Behold, the church of St Cuthbert spattered with the blood of the priests of God, despoiled of all its ornaments; a place more venerable than all in Britain is given as prey to pagan peoples.

Monasteries were easy targets for the attackers. They were full of rich pickings and their inhabitants had few means of self-defence. In the years after the first Viking attack monks lived in constant fear. This anxiety is expressed vividly in the words of an Irish monk, written in the margin of the manuscript he was working on:

Fierce and wild is the wind tonight,
It tosses the tresses of the sea to white;
On such a night I take my ease;
Fierce Norsemen only course the quiet seas.

THE MONASTERIES ARE ABANDONED

Under the impact of the Vikings all the English kingdoms except Wessex were destroyed. Monasteries near the coast were the first to be abandoned and others eventually followed. The monks of Lindisfarne gave up their dangerous coastal site, taking with them the precious relics of St Cuthbert. It was not until about 995 that the relics from Lindisfarne found a permanent home in Durham.

Some monasteries were not abandoned but the monks were replaced by clergy, known as canons. These men lived together as a community but did not follow the full routine of worship and discipline laid down by St Benedict.

English monasteries began to revive in the mid-tenth century, at a time when monasticism was undergoing a renaissance in Continental Europe. The rebirth of the English monasteries owed much to the efforts of one man, Dunstan. He was an educated man with royal connections. In about 940 King Edmund made Dunstan abbot of Glastonbury in Somerset, and allowed him to reorganise the monastic community at this ancient site. The monastic revival in England dates from this time.

Under Dunstan the abbey at Glastonbury became a renowned educational centre. Members of the royal family were frequent visitors, and royal treasure and important charters were often stored at Glastonbury for safekeeping. Dunstan himself went on to become archbishop of Glastonbury.

ABOVE *The remains of Lindisfarne Priory, Northumberland. The Viking attack on Lindisfarne in 793 shocked contemporaries and marked the beginning of the Viking Age*

ABOVE
This Anglo-Saxon book mount was ripped from a book and stolen by a Norwegian Viking. Much rich material of this kind could be found in Anglo-Saxon monasteries

TOP *The head of a Viking warrior from Sweden. Viking raids had a devastating impact on monastic life in Britain*

ABOVE *A gravestone of about 900 showing a group of warriors. Some commentators have suggested that this may depict a Viking force. Monks and nuns were unable to resist this kind of violence*

Hanc turre nembroth gigas construere. cum p confusione lingua rum migrant ide adpsal eosq igne colere docunt.

means put up with this, but when King Edgar's permission had been given, he very quickly expelled the impious blasphemers of God from the minster, and bringing monks from Abingdon, placed them there, being himself both their abbot and bishop.
(Aelfric, 'The Life of St Aethelwold')

In the years that followed, similar ejections took place in a number of great churches.

PLACES OF PRAYER AND WORK

In 970 the abbots of the revived English abbeys met together and agreed a common approach to daily life, in a document known as the *Regularis Concordia*. These guidelines were very much in keeping with the monasticism that was flourishing at the same time on the Continent. There was an emphasis on the elaborate rituals to be carried out by the monks in the abbey church. Formal prayer was clearly seen as the chief work of the monastery.

While the revived monasteries were primarily places of prayer they were also great artistic and cultural

ABOVE *This eleventh-century depiction of the Tower of Babel gives us a sense of how Anglo-Saxon builders worked. Little remains of the stone churches built during the revival of the monasteries in the late Saxon period. However, archaeology tells us that many were substantial buildings*

THE REVIVAL SPREADS

A number of able followers were attracted to Dunstan and Glastonbury. One important disciple was a talented monk named Aethelwold, who, in 954, left Glastonbury with a small body of monks to restore the derelict monastery of Abingdon in Oxfordshire. During the century that followed about 100 further monasteries were established in England.

The new monks were not without their enemies. In 964 Aethelwold ejected the canons from Winchester Cathedral and, with the help of the king, replaced them with monks from his own abbey of Abingdon. Aethelwold's biographer recounts this dramatic encounter:

Now at that time in the Old Minster there were evil-living clerics, possessed by pride, insolence and wanton behaviour. They divorced wives whom they had married unlawfully and took others, and were continually given over to gluttony and drunkenness. The holy man Aethelwold by no

LEFT *King Edgar, the patron of the monastic revival, shown in a tenth-century charter*

centres. English monks of the tenth century were particularly skilled in the illumination of manuscripts, and the quality of their work in gold and silver became renowned throughout western Europe. The monasteries also dominated the intellectual life of late Anglo-Saxon England. The greatest English writers of the period were monks: Wulfstan of York and Aelfric of Evesham. Many monks were active beyond the cloisters, not only as writers, but as teachers and advisers to the king and bishops.

BELOW *St Dunstan at the feet of Christ. Dunstan himself may have drawn this image. He was the single most important figure in the monastic revival of the tenth century*

THE NORMAN TAKEOVER

The Norman Conquest had a dramatic impact on monastic life. The invaders were a complex people: brutal and deeply religious at the same time, fierce warriors but also great builders of monasteries. Under their supervision many new abbeys were established. Norman abbots were brought over to take control of English monasteries, and everywhere existing monastic churches were replaced with new, grander buildings. The Norman character was described by a distinguished early twelfth-century monk, William of Malmesbury:

❖ The Normans are a race hardened to war, and they can hardly live without it. They are fierce when they attack their enemies, and if

ABOVE *Norman horsemen charging Harold's troops at the Battle of Hastings, from the Bayeux Tapestry. Norman knights and barons were both warlike and pious. They were great patrons of monasticism*

force fails they are ready to use trickery or bribery to get their way. After their coming to England they revived the rule of religion which had decayed. You might see new churches in every village, and, in the towns and cities, monasteries built in a style unknown before. Under the Normans, the country flourished with renewed religious observance and each wealthy man counted the day lost if he had not made some large gift to the Church.

THE IMPACT OF LANFRANC
In religious matters, William the Conqueror relied on the advice of Lanfranc, an Italian monk whom he had known at the influential Norman abbeys of Bec and Caen. Lanfranc became archbishop of Canterbury in 1070 and from then until his death in 1089 he revolutionised life in English

abbeys. He wanted to get rid of local English traditions and make the monasteries identical in worship to those of France and Italy.

Some of the English monks bitterly resented this Norman seizure of power and the threat it posed to their own traditions. At Glastonbury, for example, Lanfranc imposed a new abbot named Thurstan, who came from Lanfranc's old abbey at Caen. Thurstan's attempts to change the

forms of worship at Glastonbury led to resistance by the monks and the abbot finally resorted to armed force to make them obey:

❖ There was a disgraceful contention between the abbot of Glastonbury and his monks; so that after altercation they came to blows. The monks being driven into church bewailed their miseries at the holy altar; but the soldiers, rushing in, slew two of them, wounded fourteen and drove away the rest. *(William of Malmesbury)*

THE HEYDAY OF THE BENEDICTINE MONASTERIES
The first century after the Norman Conquest was a time of great achievement for the Benedictine monasteries of England. Apart from a few exceptions, such as Thurstan of

ABOVE *A reconstruction drawing of the building of Battle Abbey in Sussex. The new abbey buildings were consecrated in 1094 in the presence of the Conqueror's son, William Rufus. New monastic buildings such as this were erected all over England by the Normans*

RIGHT *Lanfranc, Benedictine monk and archbishop of Canterbury 1070–89. Originally from northern Italy, Lanfranc later became a monk at the leading abbey of Bec in Normandy. William the Conqueror brought him over to re-organise the English Church and he had a strong impact on English monastic life*

ABOVE *Battle Abbey today: the ruins of the dormitory buildings. This enormous communal sleeping place was, after the church itself, the largest room in the abbey*

BELOW *The official seal of Battle Abbey. The monastery was founded by William the Conqueror in 1070, on the site of the Battle of Hastings*

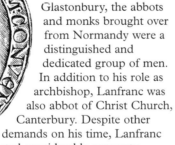

ABOVE *A reconstruction drawing of the apse and high altar of the Norman abbey church at Battle. The altar was said to be located at the spot where King Harold was slain*

Glastonbury, the abbots and monks brought over from Normandy were a distinguished and dedicated group of men. In addition to his role as archbishop, Lanfranc was also abbot of Christ Church, Canterbury. Despite other demands on his time, Lanfranc devoted considerable energy to ensuring the well-being of the monastery.

The chronicle of Gloucester Abbey shows how one energetic man could revive a monastery in decline. Abbot Serlo, a monk from Mont St Michel in Normandy, transformed the community and buildings at Gloucester, increasing the number of monks from ten in 1072 to 100 at the time of his death in 1104.

Perhaps the most successful monastery was St Albans in Hertfordshire. The abbey benefited from a series of determined and energetic abbots. The first Norman abbot of St Albans was Paul, a nephew of Lanfranc. Under his guidance, St Albans won a reputation for the high quality of its liturgy and for artistic and intellectual excellence.

The link between the power of the Norman rulers and the status of the Benedictine abbeys is clearly seen in the foundation of Battle Abbey in Sussex, on the site of the Battle of Hastings. The abbey was founded by the Conqueror himself, on the spot where King Harold was reputed to have been killed, and it was given rich gifts of land. In the early twelfth century Battle was ruled by a Norman abbot named Ralph. The chronicle of the abbey describes Ralph's character and gives a good picture of the strict monastic life followed in many of the Norman abbeys:

> He himself practised what he preached; he lived what he taught. Saying that one should hasten to the divine service, he was there before younger men even though himself aged and leaning on a staff. First in choir, he was the last to leave. He ever bent his knees in prayer though he could scarce bend them when he walked. He recited the whole of the book of psalms every day. Neither a racking cough, not haemorrhage, nor old age, nor a body shrunk to a skeleton could break him or bend him from his way of life.

THE CISTERCIAN REVOLUTION

ABOVE *Rievaulx Abbey in Yorkshire. Rievaulx was one of the first Cistercian abbeys in England and was a daughter house of the great abbey of Clairvaux in France. Its first abbot was William, an Englishman who had been living as a monk with St Bernard at Clairvaux*

I n 1098 twenty monks left the monastery of Molesme in Burgundy because they wanted to live a stricter, simpler life. They set up a new community in the forest of Cîteaux – from which the 'Cistercian' order was to take its name. An English monk named Stephen Harding was one of this pioneering group. Harding later became abbot of Cîteaux and played an important part in shaping a new approach to the monastic life. In 1111 a brilliant, charismatic young monk named Bernard arrived to join the community, together with thirty followers. Four years later Bernard set up a new Cistercian house at Clairvaux. This was one of the first of hundreds of monasteries that were established across Europe by the new order.

There were radical differences between the Cistercians and the established Benedictine monks.

✦ The Cistercian 'choir' monks spent less time attending organised services and were able to undertake more private prayer, reading and manual labour.

✦ Cistercians developed a new class of monks, known as 'lay brothers'. These were generally illiterate men from a poor background who did much of the manual work of the abbey.

✦ The Cistercians tried to simplify and purify the monastic life. They rejected any practice not mentioned in the Rule of St Benedict. As a result they banned the use of such diverse items as lard, combs, underwear and bedspreads! Their religious life was simpler than that of the Benedictines, to the point of austerity: they used iron, not gold and silver, for candlesticks, elaborate vestments were abandoned and linen robes were used in place of silk. Early Cistercian churches were simple in design with minimal decoration.

✦ The custom of accepting children as recruits was rejected. The Cistercians insisted that no person under the age of sixteen should enter the community, and that each recruit must follow a year's course as a novice before being finally accepted as a monk.

✦ Whereas a Benedictine monastery was an independent organisation, the Cistercians saw themselves, irrespective of their particular abbey, as members of a single, disciplined 'order'. Each Cistercian abbey was inspected annually by the abbot of the monastery from which its first members had come.

THE CISTERCIANS REACH ENGLAND

Between 1128 and 1132 Cistercian abbeys were established at Waverley in Surrey and at Rievaulx and Fountains in Yorkshire. In the following twenty years there was a huge expansion of Cistercian abbeys in England. The monks were inspired by a powerful idealism. Aelred, the saintly abbot of Rievaulx from 1147 to 1167, described the motives of the first Cistercian monks:

> Everywhere peace, everywhere serenity, and a marvellous freedom from the tumult of the world. Each thing seems to belong to all, and all to each. No perfection expressed in the words of the gospel is wanting to our order and our way of life.

LEFT *St Bernard, abbot of Clairvaux. He was a dominant figure in both the Cistercian revolution and the intellectual life of Europe in the twelfth century*

BELOW *A Cistercian abbot kneels in prayer before the Virgin Mary. The carving comes from the monastery at Abbey Dore in Herefordshire. Cistercians had a special devotion to the Virgin, to whom all their monasteries were dedicated*

The setting for these abbeys was often remote and sometimes spectacularly beautiful. Walter Daniel, a monk at Rievaulx, described its location:

> High hills surround the valley, encircling it like a crown. These are clothed by trees of various sorts providing for the monks a kind of second paradise of wooded delight. From the loftiest rocks the waters wind and tumble down to the valley below, and they give out a gentle murmur of soft sound and join together in the sweet notes of a delicious melody.

LAY BROTHERS
The lay brothers played an important role in the early Cistercian abbeys. They lived similar but separate lives from the choir monks, taking simpler religious vows and attending fewer church services. They were provided with large separate dormitories within the abbey complex. The lay brothers were responsible for much of the heavy manual work of the abbey. Many of them lived on granges (large farms) at some distance from the main monastic buildings, returning to the abbey on Sundays and feast days. In the later Middle Ages the Cistercians found difficulty recruiting lay brothers and the system fell into disuse.

Occasionally the lay brothers rebelled, claiming that they were

ABOVE *A contemporary depiction of Stephen Harding holding the church at Cîteaux in his hands. This Englishman played a key role in the establishment of the order*

ABOVE *A reconstruction drawing of a meeting in the chapter house at Cleeve Abbey, Somerset, in the thirteenth century. As in Benedictine monasteries, this daily business meeting took its name from a brief reading of an extract or chapter from the Rule of St Benedict*

being badly treated. In about 1206 the Cistercian abbot of Margam, in south Wales, was attacked by his lay brothers. They manhandled the cellarer off his horse and chased the abbot away from the abbey. The rebels then went on strike and refused to provide food for the choir monks. During the strike they barricaded themselves into their dormitory. When the rebellion finally came to an end the lay brothers were ordered to walk from Margam to Clairvaux in France as a penance. After this they were to be dispersed to different Cistercian monasteries. It is not known how many lay brothers actually made the journey from Wales to France on foot.

ABOVE *Cistercians saw themselves as true followers of the Rule of St Benedict. Accordingly the chanted psalms of the eight daily services or offices were at the heart of their daily round. These services were simpler than those of the Benedictines in order to make more time for private prayer, study and work*

MONASTERIES IN THE MEDIEVAL WORLD

Monks and nuns lived a life of retreat from the sin and turmoil
of the world. However, it was never possible to sever contact
completely with people living beyond the cloister.
Monasteries offered charity and hospitality to outsiders, including
pilgrims visiting their shrines. Monks and nuns also operated as
traders, landowners, counsellors and politicians.

BUSINESS AFFAIRS

ABOVE *A dispute between clergy and villagers over the payment of tithes. The villagers hold corn and livestock. These agricultural products were the basis of wealth in the Middle Ages and were central to the economic life of medieval abbeys*

BELOW *The fourteenth-century Luttrell Psalter shows a laden wagon being pushed uphill, with some difficulty. Large Benedictine monasteries required substantial numbers of servants and labourers in order to sustain the spiritual work of the community*

The first European monasteries had simple economic requirements and sought to be as self-sufficient as possible. St Benedict ordered that a monastery should have a mill, a garden and various workshops within the abbey precinct so that the monks rarely needed to leave the monastery. He expected that monks would perform manual labour themselves and anticipated that some of them would be skilled craftsmen. Despite the general simplicity of the Rule, however, St Benedict also assumed that, unless they were extremely poor, monasteries would have servants to do much of the labouring.

> If the circumstances of the place or their poverty require them to gather the harvest themselves, let them not be discontented: for then they are truly monks when they live by the labour of their hands, like our fathers and the apostles.

In the following centuries the use of servants increased considerably. By the time of the monastic revival of the tenth century monastic life had become more elaborate, and was supported by complex economic arrangements. In large communities the monks spent much more time in church and less on manual labour. It was therefore necessary to employ many lay servants and to generate a substantial income to pay for the

upkeep of the community. As a result, larger abbeys teemed with servants, craftsmen and labourers. At Canterbury in 1322, for example, the cellarer alone had the following staff:

the steward of the guesthouse and two porters;
the keeper of the pantry and his boy;
the keeper of the cloister-gate and his boy;
the keeper of the guesthouse pantry;
the watchman;
the scullion and his boy;
the soup maker;
the scullion of the refectory and his boy;
the first and second cooks and their boys;
the salter and his boy;
the kitchen stoker;
the potter;
the kitchen waiter;
the drawer of wine and beer and his boy;
the cellarer's esquire;
the cellarer's groom;
the cellarer's carter;
two purveyors;
the hunter and his boy;
the porter of the guesthouse and his boy;
a general servant;
the gaoler.

BUILDINGS FOR AGRICULTURE AND INDUSTRY

Feeding a large community required considerable organisation. Extensive granaries were built within the abbey precinct for the storage of corn. A large bakehouse was needed for bread-making. The demands of a meat-free diet led to the creation of extensive fish ponds. In the later Middle Ages much of the economic

BELOW *A villager brings corn to a windmill, in a carving from the Cistercian abbey at Rievaulx. Mills were a useful source of revenue for monastic landlords because tenants were obliged to pay a fee for the privilege of using them*

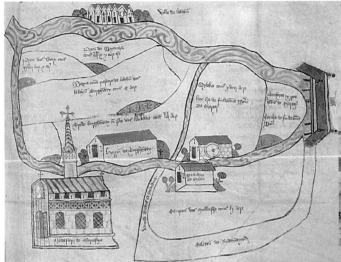

life of a great monastery took place in an area beyond the church and cloisters known as the outer court. The buildings of the outer court were usually a mixture of the agricultural and the industrial. At Rievaulx, for example, the outer court contained a large tannery and the workshops of the abbey's smiths and plumbers. Many outer courts also included a dovecote: pigeons were a useful source of fresh meat and pigeon droppings were carefully collected for use in the treatment of parchment.

A corn mill was often to be found in the outer court. These were almost always operated by water, and the availability of a good mill-stream was sometimes an important factor in the location of an abbey. The most impressive surviving water-mill is that of Fountains Abbey in Yorkshire, which remained in use until 1937.

INCOME AND EXPENDITURE

Abbeys varied considerably in wealth. Towards the end of the Middle Ages the rich Benedictine abbey of Glastonbury enjoyed an income 100 times greater than the small Benedictine abbey of Humberston in Lincolnshire. Even large abbeys were often in debt. Until their expulsion from England, Jewish bankers were frequently involved in the financial affairs of monasteries. Before his death, the great twelfth-century financier Aaron of Lincoln was owed a huge 6,400 marks by nine Cistercian abbeys, including Rievaulx. He also lent large sums to Benedictine houses. The chronicle of St Albans notes that in 1183 Aaron was living at the abbey

and made a contribution to the building of the shrine of the abbey's patron saint.

The expenses of a large community were considerable. In one week in 1432 the kitchen of Durham Cathedral Priory used 22 sheep, 5 cattle, 2 calves, 13 piglets, 400 eggs and a cartload of fish. At the same time the monks of Durham were buying large quantities of wine from the merchants of Newcastle. A huge sum, about 20 per cent of the community's income, was spent on wheat and barley. The barley was used to make a weak beer, the most common drink for medieval people, which was consumed by monks and nuns in enormous quantities. The Cistercian monks of Beaulieu Abbey in Hampshire had an allowance of a gallon of ale a day, a common level of consumption. At Bolton Priory in Yorkshire the canons, their servants and guests drank a total of about 50,000 gallons a year. This huge consumption of beer made necessary the building of substantial brewhouses as well as kilns for malting barley.

FARMS AND GRANGES

In medieval times wealth and power were, to a large extent, associated with the ownership of land and the monasteries were great landowners. Perhaps as much as one-seventh of all land in England was in monastic hands in the late Middle Ages. There was a traditional saying that 'if the abbot of Glastonbury could marry the abbess of Shaftesbury, their heir would hold more land than the king of England'.

The way in which monasteries managed their land varied over time. It could either be leased out to others in return for rent, or managed directly by members of the community. In the twelfth and thirteenth centuries the direct administration of land grew more popular and leading monks and nuns became heavily involved in the business side of agriculture. Growth in the population, rising prices and the development of new markets meant that there were considerable profits to be made by energetic monastic landowners. Members of monastic communities began to appreciate that much extra money could be made by taking land 'in hand' as leases came to an end.

The thirteenth century was a time of great achievement in English agriculture and many monasteries pioneered new farming methods on their estates. Records from Canterbury Cathedral Priory, for example, show the prior building sea-

defences and new farm buildings and experimenting in the latest farming techniques in order to improve the yield.

THE CISTERCIANS: A NEW APPROACH

As landowners most monks and nuns were part of the feudal system. The hard manual work of farming was done by unfree 'villeins' – poor villagers who were obliged to work for the monastery as the owner of the manor. The Cistercians, by contrast, had no wish to be encumbered with manors and villeins. Instead, they wanted land that could be worked largely by the lay brothers of the community, outside the manorial system. On occasion, this led to the Cistercians evicting existing communities of villeins on newly acquired land. These methods were not without their critics. In about 1180 Walter Map, a royal courtier, wrote a vitriolic attack on Cistercian farming. As evidence of the monks' hypocrisy he cited the fact that they were strict vegetarians but were quite happy to raise thousands of pigs and chickens. He darkly suggested that perhaps some of them secretly ate meat from their own farms. He criticised the custom of clearing land – and even destroying existing villages – to make way for new monasteries:

> They are ordered to live in desert places, and desert places they either

ABOVE *An illuminated initial from St Albans Abbey showing sheep-shearing. English wool was a highly profitable export for much of the Middle Ages and monastic landlords made good profits through sheep farming*

BELOW *Men and women reaping. Monastic farmland was frequently leased to lay people in return for rent, but direct management by the monastery could be more profitable*

find or make. Their rule does not allow them to have ordinary lay people on their land, so they destroy villages and churches, evict the people and plough up their settlements.

MONKS AND THE WOOL TRADE

Monastic farms were often known as granges. Cistercian monasteries had an elaborate system of granges, many of which specialised in sheep-farming. The remote areas settled by the first Cistercians were often ideal for sheep-rearing and Cistercian monks played an important part in the English wool trade.

Whilst a great Cistercian abbey such as Fountains in Yorkshire drew income from many sources, the most valuable of its products was wool. By the end of the thirteenth century the sale of wool generated three times as much money for the abbey as any other source of income. At this time Fountains probably owned about 15,000 sheep. Enormous sheep runs were developed on the moors and fells of the Pennines. Every year the sheep would be brought down to the granges in the valleys and lowlands where the shearing took place. From the granges the clip was taken to Fountains itself, where it was initially stored in a great wool-house within the abbey complex. The wool was later transported to the towns of York and Boston, for sale to merchants.

The Cistercians were undoubtedly great sheep-farmers but they were not the only monastic order that produced large quantities of wool. The wealthy Augustinians of Ciren-cester and the Benedictines of Winchcombe produced much of the Cotswold wool that was highly prized by Continental wool merchants.

THE END OF AN ERA

Agriculture was badly affected by a series of crises in the fourteenth century, including poor harvests, pestilence amongst livestock and a catastrophic collapse in the size of the human population as a result of the Black Death. This last factor contributed to a further dislocation of the economy of the Cistercian order, which was unable to recruit lay brothers to work on the granges of its great abbeys. Faced with these problems monasteries began to abandon direct involvement in agriculture; once again, they leased out their lands. In the 1390s even Canterbury Cathedral Priory, which had been so energetic in its agricultural policy in the previous century, abandoned direct administration in favour of rent collection.

BELOW *A reconstruction drawing of the wool-house at Fountains Abbey in the fourteenth century. The abbey became the largest single producer of wool in the north of England. Much of the produce was brought from outlying granges to this central wool-house, located in the abbey precinct, before being taken to market*

BELOW *The granges of Fountains Abbey, one of the great Cistercian houses of Yorkshire. Some of the granges were created by the eviction of existing villagers*

F Fountains and the home granges
■ Granges
• Vills (settlements) in which Fountains held land

Whitby
Richmond
Skipton
Harrogate
York
Leeds

RIGHT *Shepherds at work and play as they tend their flocks*

THE GIVING OF ALMS

RIGHT *A fourteenth-century manuscript showing a Benedictine monk offering food and drink to a traveller. St Benedict had placed great emphasis on the importance of hospitality*

ABOVE *The gatehouse of Kirkham Priory, Yorkshire. In the late Middle Ages the Augustinians of Kirkham provided accommodation – at a price – to a large number of elderly men*

From the time of St Benedict monasteries recognised that they had a responsibility to give alms or charity to the local poor. The monastic official known as the almoner provided the link between a monastery and the poor. In the eleventh century Archbishop Lanfranc provided instructions for the work of the almoner. His duties entailed visiting the houses of the sick and poor in order to find out what help was needed. Before he entered any house all the women were obliged to leave. He was not allowed to visit sick women but sent them money or food through an intermediary.

A later view of the duties of an almoner, this time from an Augustinian source, is provided by a document known as the 'Customs of Barnwell':

❖ Old men and those who are decrepit, lame and blind or who are confined to their beds, he ought frequently to visit and give them suitable relief. Those who in former days have been rich, and have come to poverty, and are perhaps ashamed to sit down among the rest, he will assemble them separately that he may distribute his bounty to them with greater privacy. He ought to submit with calmness to the loud-voiced importunity of the poor and help all petitioners as far as

he is able. He ought not to strike or hurt or even abuse anyone, always remembering that they are made in the image of God.

A PLACE OF REFUGE
In the early Middle Ages monasteries provided emergency assistance during turbulent times. Shortly after the Conquest there was a rebellion against Norman rule in the north of England. This was crushed with great brutality by William the Conqueror. Many people were killed and villages burnt. The chronicle of Evesham Abbey tells how refugees from the North flocked to Evesham and sought help from the abbot, Aethelwig:

❖ A vast multitude of men old and young, and of women with their little ones, came to Evesham even in their distress, fleeing from famine; all these Aethelwig supported as best he could. Many, who had long been starving, died after eating ravenously, and the wretches lay sick throughout the town, indoors and out and even in our cemetery, starving and dying when they ate. And thus many died for many days, so that five or six daily, sometimes more, who thus died miserably, were buried here by the prior.

ABOVE *The 'sanctuary' door knocker from Durham Cathedral Priory. During the Middle Ages those in trouble with the law could seek sanctuary in the consecrated grounds of a church. Fugitives in sanctuary were sometimes allowed to escape punishment if they agreed to leave the country and go into exile*

LEFT *Fifteenth-century stained-glass windows from York showing the giving of water to the thirsty. For fervent monks and nuns acts of charity, such as this, were part of their attempt to imitate Christ*

CHARITY AT A WEALTHY NUNNERY

The amount that was given to the poor varied from place to place. A late thirteenth-century document lists all the almsgiving at the relatively wealthy nunnery of Lacock in Wiltshire:

❖ ALMS GIVEN BY THE NUNS OF LACOCK:
✦ On All Souls' Day a number of poor people were fed equal to the number of sisters at the abbey. Each poor person was given a loaf of bread and either two herrings or a slice of cheese.
✦ On the anniversary of the death of the founder (Ela, Countess of Salisbury, 24 August 1261) 100 poor people were each given a good wheaten loaf and two herrings.
✦ On the anniversary of the death of the founder's father and on that of her husband's death, thirteen poor people were fed.
✦ Whenever one of the nuns died 100 poor people were given either a small sum of money or a loaf.
✦ On Maundy Thursday every poor person was entitled to a loaf of the best quality, half a gallon of beer, two herrings and half a bushel of beans for soup.

ALMSGIVING ON MAUNDY THURSDAY

The most important day for almsgiving in most monasteries was Maundy Thursday, the occasion on which the Last Supper was remembered. This was a traditional time for the giving of clothes, food and money to the poor and for the ritual washing of the feet of a number of poor men and women. Precise instructions for the washing of feet on Maundy Thursday have survived from Canterbury Cathedral Priory. The almoner was responsible for gathering together a group of poor men from the town. Before entering the cloister, however, the poor had to wash their own feet! This meant that the monks' washing which followed was a purely symbolic act. The poor men were lined up in the cloister and each monk was allotted a particular poor man. When the prior gave the signal all the monks knelt down and carried out the ritual ablution:

❖ And bowing down they shall adore Christ in the poor. Each one shall wash the feet of his poor man, wipe and kiss them, and touch them with his forehead.

ABOVE *Visiting those in prison. While a strict interpretation of the Rule of St Benedict allowed only rare journeys from the monastery, the almoner had special permission to leave the precinct in order to carry out his charitable duties*

BELOW *The almonry at Cleeve Abbey, Somerset, was located in the gatehouse. The poor would come here to receive alms. A Latin inscription above the gate reads, in translation, 'Gate be open, shut to no honest person'*

After the ceremony the poor were given a drink and some money.

A CASE OF 'CHARITY BEGINS AT HOME'?

Some almoners do not appear to have taken their charitable work very seriously. The almoner at Canterbury Cathedral Priory was in receipt of a large income. He had his own servants and was in charge of a whole complex of almonry buildings. Whilst he did distribute some food from the abbey's farms to the poor, the almoner gave away only a tiny fraction of money as charity. Between 1284 and 1373 he spent a remarkably low 0.5 per cent of all his revenues on alms. Far more of the revenue was used for buying treats for the other monks, while the bulk of the money was spent on the almoner's own expenses and the cost of his servants.

A similar picture appears from a study of the almoner at Bolton Priory in Yorkshire. Here the amount spent on presents to the rich and powerful far exceeded the money given to the poor. A small amount of food was regularly distributed to the poor, but of this the quantity of corn given between 1298 and 1304 was less than that fed to the abbey's pack of hounds. Some of the money gifts to the 'poor' were questionable: in 1314 the sister and niece of the wealthy Dean of York were given charity, and the following year the prior's nephew received a large amount in alms.

LEFT *Visiting the sick. The order of Augustinian canons had a particular reputation for its pastoral work among the sick. Many medieval hospitals were founded by monastic orders*

ABOVE *Christ washes the feet of the apostles during the Last Supper. This act of humility was re-enacted every year during the Maundy Thursday rituals. Poor people were brought into monasteries and their feet were washed; afterwards they were given alms*

PATRONAGE AND BENEFACTORS

had a direct line of communication with God and would regularly pray for their benefactors, who, through the monks' mediation, would eventually be able to reach heaven.

THE BENEFITS OF PATRONAGE

One Benedictine monk explained to a nobleman the benefits of founding a monastery as follows:

❖ Look carefully at the things that are provided for you by trained monks living in monasteries under a Rule: strenuous is the warfare which these castle-guards of Christ wage against the Devil; innumerable are the benefits of their struggle. Who can recount the vigils, hymns, psalms, prayers, alms and daily offerings of masses which the monks perform? These followers of Christ crucify themselves that they may please God. And so noble earl, I earnestly advise you to build such a castle in your

Many kings and nobles were keen to establish monasteries in the early Middle Ages and were ready to give huge amounts of land to support monastic communities. These men were warriors and they looked on monks as their spiritual counterparts – as 'soldiers for Christ'. While knights fought the enemy of their feudal lord, monks fought the enemies of God through prayer and self-discipline. This sense of monasticism as a kind of military life is clear from the writings of twelfth-century monks. Bernard of Clairvaux, for example, called his fellow Cistercians 'new soldiers for Christ':

❖ In your country there is a prize of my Lord's and yours which I am resolved to seize by sending our force of knights. For this purpose I have sent forward these men to reconnoitre. Assist them therefore as officers of your Lord and fulfil through them your feudal service.
(Bernard of Clairvaux writing to Henry I)

Patrons of monasteries were hard-headed, powerful men. A gift to a monastery was seen as a shrewd investment. The soldiers for Christ

ABOVE *Henry III ensured that the finest craftsmen of the time were employed on Westminster Abbey*

ABOVE RIGHT *The fourteenth-century gatehouse of the Augustinian Butley Priory, Suffolk. The façade of the gatehouse was covered with the coats of arms of patrons*

RIGHT *The benefactors' book of Tewkesbury Abbey, Gloucestershire. The monks showed their gratitude to this patron, Isabella le Despenser, by praying for her soul and including her portrait in this list of friends of the abbey*

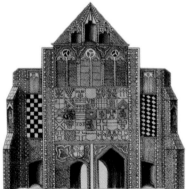

country, manned by monks against Satan. Here the cowled champions will resist the Devil in constant warfare for your soul.
(Orderic Vitalis)

FASHIONS IN PATRONAGE

Patrons were attracted to those monks and nuns whose prayers were most likely to be effective. In the eleventh century the Benedictine abbey of Cluny in France had a reputation for elaborate ritual and almost constant prayer. By the early twelfth century the style of Cluny was less fashionable. New orders emerged that attempted to establish a simpler, purer way of life and these in turn attracted the patronage of the rich and powerful. Between 1100 and 1130 there was a sudden surge in popularity of communities of Augustinian canons. They combined a life of worship with, in some cases, pastoral care for local people and the maintenance of hospitals. From the 1130s fashions changed again and many patrons were keen to support the new Cistercians because of their reputation for sanctity.

that they did not require large gifts of land. A relatively small gift of a group of houses and garden in a town was enough to set up a friary.

While the number of new foundations declined steeply in the later Middle Ages patrons remained attracted to those monks and nuns who maintained high standards. The small but extremely strict Carthusian order received substantial patronage in the fourteenth century.

LEFT *Sir Geoffrey Luttrell with his wife and daughter-in-law. There were many links between the nobility and the monastic world: one of Sir Geoffrey's daughters, Isabella, became a nun at the Gilbertine monastery at Sempringham in Lincolnshire, of which the Luttrell family had long been patrons*

ABOVE *A fourteenth-century nobleman entertains two Dominican friars. The nobleman is Sir Geoffrey Luttrell. In his will he made gifts not only to the Dominicans but also to Gilbertines, Cistercians, Augustinians, Franciscans and Carmelites*

FAR RIGHT *A tiled pavement from Cleeve Abbey in Somerset shows the coat of arms of the Clare family, benefactors of this Cistercian community*

One of the barons of Henry I, Walter Espec, was typical of the great patrons of the twelfth century. At first he supported the Augustinians and helped to found the Yorkshire priory of Kirkham in about 1122. In 1132, Espec provided land in Yorkshire for the pioneering Cistercian abbey of Rievaulx, situated close to his own castle at Helmsley. When the community at Rievaulx began to expand Espec gave them further land for a 'daughter house' at Warden in Bedfordshire.

Patterns of patronage changed once more in the thirteenth century. The new orders of friars were now seen as the most saintly. For benefactors, the friars had the additional advantage

SHRINES AND PILGRIMS

Most monasteries possessed the relics of saints and these were treated as great treasures. To the medieval mind, saints were those holy men and women who had gained a place in heaven and, being close to God, had the power to help people who prayed to them. A relic – part of a saint's body or property once owned by a saint – was thought to have special power. Relics were greatly prized and different monasteries occasionally argued over ownership. The bones of the most revered saints were sometimes divided up so that several great churches could share the relic. Thus, in the tenth century, the head of St Oswald was kept in Norham in Northumberland, while one arm was at Bamburgh and the rest of the body in Gloucester.

The Cistercian abbey at Hailes in Gloucestershire claimed to have an exceptional relic. In the thirteenth century Edmund, Earl of Cornwall presented the abbey with a vial purported to contain the blood of Christ. He claimed to have discovered the blood during his travels in Germany. Even at the time there was a debate in the Church as to whether or not the blood could be genuine. Despite these doubts, the blood became a focus for pilgrimage and Hailes Abbey attracted many visitors in the centuries that followed. In the sixteenth century, when the monasteries were dissolved, the blood was denounced as a hoax and destroyed.

Pilgrims often gave valuable donations to abbeys. Sometimes the donations failed to live up to expectations, however. Jocelin of Brakelond, the chronicler of Bury St Edmunds Abbey, was unimpressed by the generosity of one royal pilgrim:

King John came straight to the Abbey of St Edmund immediately after his coronation. The monks believed that he would make a great donation to the Abbey; but the only thing he gave was a cloth of silk which his servants had borrowed from our Sacrist, and which was never paid for. At the same time he was entertained by the Abbey at great cost, and when he left his only gift was thirteen pence.

ABOVE *Illustration from a thirteenth-century biography of Edward the Confessor. Edward was viewed as a saint, and Westminster Abbey was the focus for pilgrims who wished to pray before his relics*

CARE OF PILGRIMS

Certain members of a monastic community would have a particular responsibility for dealing with pilgrims. The care of relics was the duty of the sacrist, who would also organise the collection of donations from pilgrims. The guest-master was charged with providing accommodation for important visitors, including pilgrims. Lanfranc in the eleventh century described how the guest-master should show visitors round the abbey. Those wearing unsuitable clothes were clearly not welcome:

His duty it is to show the buildings to those who want to see them, taking care that the community is not then sitting in the cloister. He shall not introduce into the cloister under any circumstances anyone wearing riding-boots or spurs, nor anyone who goes barefoot or only has drawers on his legs.

ABOVE *An imaginative reconstruction of Hailes Abbey in about 1300. Pilgrims kneel in front of the shrine of the Holy Blood, while monks stand in attendance. Such a relic was a great asset to a monastery*

BELOW *The Holy Blood is carried through the streets of London in 1247, accompanied by Henry III. This was the relic later housed at Hailes Abbey. The drawing was the work of the Benedictine monk, Matthew Paris, who was an eye-witness of the procession*

THE CANTERBURY TALES

In England the greatest shrine of the Middle Ages was that of Thomas Becket, the martyred archbishop of Canterbury. At a major shrine, such as Canterbury, the gifts of pilgrims constituted a very lucrative source of revenue for the abbey. In the late fourteenth century (the time of Chaucer's fictional pilgrimage) donations averaged over £500 a year. In medieval terms this was a fabulous amount of money, far exceeding the income more ordinary abbeys earned from all their landed estates. The level of donations declined in the fifteenth century, but until that time gifts from pilgrims constituted one quarter of all the income of this extremely wealthy monastery.

In his *Canterbury Tales* Chaucer made fun of both relics and pilgrims to the great shrine at Canterbury. He does not appear to have held the monastic life in high esteem – indeed monks and nuns were coming under increasing criticism generally at this time. The great majority of Chaucer's imaginary pilgrims are worldly people with little religious motivation. For them the pilgrimage is little more than the excuse for a holiday. One of their number, the Pardoner, is a trickster who dupes poor country people into buying worthless fake relics: his bag contains a pillow-case which he claims to be a veil of the Virgin Mary, a piece of sail alleged to come from St Peter's boat, and a glass container full of pigs' bones. The other pilgrims include a monk, a friar and a prioress, all of whom lead far from saintly personal lives. The prioress is a foolish woman, concerned more with her pet dogs than religion. The friar is a money-grabbing womaniser. The monk keeps hunting-dogs and lives like a lord.

A pilgrim visiting the shrine of St Thomas in 1538, shortly before its destruction, described how the prior opened a case in order to show him the head of St Thomas. He invited the pilgrim to kneel and kiss the head, saying three times, 'This is St Thomas's head'. The visitor, although impressed by the great richness of the shrine, was less taken with the relic and declined the prior's invitation.

ABOVE *Pilgrimage was an international business. This pilgrim badge from Amiens in France was found at Maison Dieu Hospital in Kent. It shows the relic of the head of John the Baptist which was said to be kept at Amiens*

ABOVE *This pilgrim token was a souvenir of a visit to the shrine of St Thomas*

LEFT *The shrine of St Thomas at Canterbury was the single most important pilgrimage site in late medieval England. In this painting of about 1200 the monks of Canterbury place Becket in his tomb*

BELOW *A casket designed to hold some of St Thomas's relics. It was made in about 1200 and is decorated with scenes of the saint's martyrdom*

DURHAM
St Cuthbert

WALSINGHAM
Our Lady

ST ALBANS
St Alban

BURY ST
EDMUNDS
St Edmund

HAILES
Holy Blood

LONDON
St Edward
the Confessor

GLASTONBURY
St Dunstan

CANTERBURY
St Thomas

ABOVE *A sixteenth-century illustration of Chaucer's pilgrims en route to the shrine of St Thomas at Canterbury*

LEFT *Some of the major pilgrim centres in later medieval England, and the relics associated with them* **49**

MONASTIC BOROUGHS

ABOVE *Aerial view of St Albans today showing the monastic church and the surrounding town. There was often tension between the monks of St Albans and the people of the town*

Many monks and nuns regarded monasteries as places of refuge from the wickedness of the world. For this reason monasteries were often established in remote places, away from the temptations of urban life. Despite this, many abbeys in medieval England came to have a neighbouring town. Monasteries that were initially located in the countryside soon attracted traders and shopkeepers to their gates and before long fully-fledged towns had sprung up. Examples of these monastic towns include such places as Abingdon, Evesham, Hartlepool, Peterborough and St Albans.

Between the eleventh and the thirteenth centuries monastic communities often deliberately laid out new town streets and invited lay-people to be their neighbours. The motive for this early town planning was the profit that could be made from rents and taxes on trade in the town market. The towns benefited in many ways from their monastic neighbours: for example, the monastery was a source of employment and poor relief. However, the local abbot often had control over aspects of local government and this sometimes led to tension with the townspeople.

We get a glimpse of the power of the abbey from an incident at Bury St Edmunds in the late twelfth century. The abbot's servants and the men of the town met at Christmas in the abbey cemetery for wrestling matches. The wrestling got out of hand and some people were badly hurt. The abbot was furious and ordered all the guilty men to come before him. Over 100 men were excommunicated for the sacrilege of fighting within the monastery precinct. Even though it was the middle of winter, this crowd was ordered to lie naked 'except for their drawers' outside the church door before the abbot would consider forgiving them. They were then all whipped.

Friction between monks and the people of the town led to several outbreaks of violence in the thirteenth and fourteenth centuries. One of the worst years for trouble in the monastic boroughs was 1327. There were armed rebellions at a number of major towns, including Barnstaple, Canterbury, Cirencester, Coventry, Dunstable and Plymouth.

REBELLIONS AT BURY ST EDMUNDS AND ABINGDON

Some of the most serious disturbances of 1327 took place at Bury St Edmunds. According to chroniclers about 3000 people, angered by the power of the abbey, stormed and ransacked the

ABOVE *The climax of the 1381 Peasants' Revolt: the rebel leader, Wat Tyler is slain and the young king, Richard II, persuades the rebels to disperse. Despite its name, the uprising also involved many townsfolk. Some of the most violent episodes of the revolt came from the monastic boroughs of Bury St Edmunds and St Albans*

LEFT *A church under attack, from a fourteenth-century manuscript. The attackers are clerks in holy orders! In 1327 the clerks of Oxford joined forces with the people of Abingdon in order to attack the local Benedictine monastery*

monastic buildings. The monks were finally rescued by the armed men of the sheriff of Norfolk. Some of the leading rebels were executed. A few months later the people of Abingdon tried to storm their abbey. The first attempt failed, so they went to Oxford for reinforcements. With help from some Oxford scholars, the mob broke down the gates and plundered the abbey. Some of the monks jumped into the Thames in order to escape the fury of the crowd. The sheriffs of Oxford and Berkshire sent forces to crush the revolt and the ring-leaders were again executed.

THE PEASANTS' REVOLT

Conflict between townsfolk and monks surfaced again in 1381 during the chaos of the so-called Peasants' Revolt. This term is something of a misnomer because the people of the towns, as well as the rural villeins, played an important part in the rebellion. There was particularly serious unrest in St Albans. Some of the people of the town went to London to join forces with the peasants of Kent and Essex. They then returned to St Albans intending to force the abbot to grant them greater freedom. There was panic in the monastery at the news that the rebellious townsfolk were on their way. The prior and four other monks decided to run for their lives. They took refuge in the priory of the abbey at Tynemouth, in distant Northumberland. The abbot himself stood his ground and met the townspeople in the abbey church. Negotiations between abbot and people were interrupted by the news from London that Wat Tyler, the leader of the rising, had been killed. The St Albans rebels lost heart after this. The government must have been especially worried by the commotion at St Albans because a few weeks later the king himself came to the monastery as part of the process of crushing the rebellion. The leaders of the townspeople were arrested and fifteen of them were executed.

VIOLENCE AT BURY

The great Benedictine abbey at Bury St Edmunds was also at the centre of a violent storm during the Peasants' Revolt. The abbey suffered more

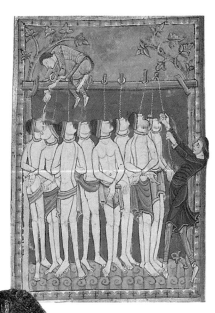

damage than any other monastery in the country. The leader of the townsfolk at Bury was a certain John Wraw. Wraw and other ring-leaders were ultimately executed. During the revolt the rebels of Bury used great violence against their enemies:

The mob captured Lord John Cavendish, Chief Justice of the Kingdom, beheaded him and shamefully placed his head on the pillory in the market place of Bury St Edmunds. They suddenly captured the prior of Bury St Edmunds while he was striving to escape from them and cruelly executed him. The prior, John de Cambridge, was a worthy and artistic man. He had taken care to fight for his monastery's rights against the people of Bury and he was killed near the town of Mildenhall. His body was stripped to his shirt and his drawers; and he lay unburied in an open field for five days.

The mob entered the town of Bury and marched round as if in procession, carrying the prior's head high on a lance in full view of the townsmen until they reached the pillory. In recognition of the previous friendship between the prior and John Cavendish and to pour scorn on both, they held together the two heads on the tops of the lances as if they were talking or kissing each other. *(Thomas of Walsingham, 'Historia Anglicana')*

THE WORLD OF POLITICS

The great abbeys were caught up in the power politics of their day. Leading abbots were members of the House of Lords, and kings, queens and barons were frequent visitors to monasteries. Visits to monastic houses were not always voluntary: nunneries were often used by the king to incarcerate the female relatives of his enemies. Having the status of a great feudal noble, the abbot of a large monastery would have regular dealings with the king. The larger abbeys were sources of both taxation and hospitality to the royal family.

In the early Middle Ages many monks left the cloister to become bishops and, in effect, civil servants. One notable example of a monk who ended his career in government service was Ealdred, the eleventh-century archbishop of York. Ealdred began as a monk at Winchester and served as abbot of Tavistock before being made a bishop. His reputation for efficiency led to an invitation by Edward the Confessor to carry out government business. Ealdred was clearly tactful and skilful. After Edward's death in 1066 he remained in government service under Harold and William the Conqueror. He acted as an international representative of the English government, twice making official trips to Germany and Rome. In 1058 Ealdred travelled to Jerusalem via Hungary: he had come a long way from the cloister at Winchester.

KING VERSUS POPE

The reign of King John (1199–1216) was a time of great tension between the Church and the royal government. John argued with the Pope, who placed a papal ban on all church services for several years. The king used this dispute as a pretext for the extortion of considerable funds from monasteries. St Albans Abbey was ordered by the king to defy the papal ban and continue with the regular celebration of the mass. The abbot refused, saying 'One should obey God rather than man; we shall have to put up with the prince's anger'. When he heard this John was furious and sent his own men to take over the running of the abbey. The abbey was only left alone when the abbot offered to pay the enormous sum of 600 marks.

AN INFLUENTIAL MONK

The connection between the monastic world and great politics is seen in the writings of Matthew Paris, a monk of St Albans. Paris moved in high circles: he knew King Henry III personally and was at the royal court on more than one occasion. St Albans provided regular hospitality to the wealthy and powerful. It was a resting place for those travelling north from London since it was positioned at one day's horse ride from the capital. The stable for guests could accommodate as many as 300 horses. During Paris's lifetime we know that Henry III stayed at St Albans no fewer than nine times.

EASY TARGETS

From the time of the earliest Viking raids onwards monasteries were often attacked during periods of political turmoil. Northern monasteries were badly affected by the periodic warfare

ABOVE *The tomb of King John, Worcester Cathedral. Like many kings, John had a stormy relationship with the Church. His financial problems led him to extort money from many great feudal landlords, including the largest monasteries*

ABOVE *English monasteries in the Middle Ages were part of the international Catholic Church. This papal 'bull' or seal came from a letter sent from Pope Honorius III (1216–27) to Thornholme Priory in Yorkshire*

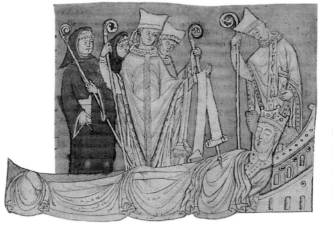

LEFT *Henry I is attacked by angry bishops and abbots. This twelfth-century drawing depicts part of a dream of the king in which he is successively confronted by peasants, knights and prelates. The drawing was made by a monk of Worcester Cathedral Priory*

between England and Scotland. This had a particularly disruptive impact on monastic life in the borders during the late twelfth and early thirteenth centuries.

A canon of the Augustinian priory of Lanercost in Cumbria indignantly recorded details of the great raid of 1296 in which his own house was burnt down:

Yorkshire was struck particularly badly in the early fourteenth century. In 1314 the Scots, led by Robert the Bruce, defeated the English at Bannockburn. Flushed by victory, they then raided the estates of the priory. Shortly afterwards, the priory lands were ravaged by a great cattle disease or murrain. The crisis became so bad that in 1320 the community

ABOVE *Although they could be the victims of political conflict, the monasteries also enjoyed special powers. This fifteenth-century ceremonial sword, from Battle Abbey, Sussex, symbolised the power of life and death that the abbot possessed over local people, and the privileges granted to the abbey by William the Conqueror*

ABOVE *Lanercost Priory, Cumbria. This Augustinian house, like many monastic houses in northern England, was devastated during the wars with Scotland in the thirteenth and fourteenth centuries. In 1320 the canons temporarily abandoned the priory as a result of war damage*

LEFT *Edward I and leading churchmen in about 1285. The abbots of the most distinguished monastic houses moved in elevated circles and were familiar with royalty and other powerful people*

❖ The Scots burnt consecrated churches. They violated women dedicated to God as well as married women and girls, either murdering them or robbing them, after gratifying their lust. Three monasteries were destroyed by them, Lanercost and Hexham and that of the nuns of Lambley. The attackers showed themselves to be not warriors, but dastardly thieves, who attacked a weaker community, where they would not be likely to meet with any resistance.

Many northern monasteries were temporarily disbanded during the chaos of the Scottish raids. The Augustinian priory of Bolton in

temporarily abandoned the priory. The archbishop of York wrote to other Augustinian houses asking them to shelter the canons during the emergency:

❖ The monastery of Bolton in Craven is in these days much devastated, because of the hostile incursion of the Scots, who of late have plundered their animals and have destroyed their villages with fire and flame, as well as the universally calamitous murrain of beasts which has long persisted in this kingdom. Its own resources are no longer sufficient to provide for the maintenance of the college of canons serving God there and for the support of the usual burdens of hospitality.

THE FRIARS' MISSION TO THE PEOPLE

In the thirteenth century a completely new religious movement reached England from the Continent. The friars rejected the enclosed traditions of the existing orders and had a much greater level of contact with ordinary people.

The first Franciscan friars arrived at Dover on 10 September 1224. They were followers of the charismatic Italian preacher, Francis of Assisi. Franciscan houses or friaries were quickly established in Canterbury, London and Oxford, the leading centres of religious, political and educational thinking. Within a few years the friars had established themselves as a powerful force in the religious and intellectual life of the country.

The arrival of the Franciscans was quite different from the coming of the Cistercians 100 years before. The white monks had sought

RIGHT *A friar preaching, from a fourteenth-century manuscript. Benedictines and Cistercians had emphasised the importance of escaping from the world; by contrast, the first friars were not confined to a monastery and saw it as their job to take the word of God to the people*

described the lifestyle of the first recruit in England, Brother Solomon:

❖ One winter he was suffering so severely from the cold and exposure that he thought he was going to die. The brethren had no way of warming him, but holy charity showed them a tender way of helping him. So all the friars gathered closely around him, warming him with the heat of their own bodies just as pigs do.

out wild and remote places for their abbeys. The Franciscans went straight to the greatest centres of population and influence. The differences between the Franciscans and the older orders were profound. The friars were not monks. They did not follow an ancient monastic rule and were not bound for life to one abbey. Their mission was not one of prayer and meditation away from the world; instead, they were committed to spreading the Christian message through preaching in the world to ordinary people. Francis and many of his early followers were passionately devoted to the idea of imitating Christ through living a life of complete poverty. Owning nothing, they survived through begging.

A Franciscan named Thomas Eccleston recorded the extreme poverty of the first English friars in a chronicle written in the 1250s. He

The Franciscans were not the only friars. A Spaniard named Dominic Guzman, who lived at about the same time as Francis, founded the order now known as the Dominicans. They developed in southern France as part of the Catholic Church's battle against heretics. The Dominicans put a particular emphasis on the importance of preaching and pastoral care.

The friars aroused some hostility from the established orders of monks. Many idealistic young men who would have joined the Benedictines or the Cistercians in earlier years now turned to the friars. The hostile attitude of the monks to the friars is seen in the chronicles of the St Albans monk, Matthew Paris. Writing in the 1230s he criticised the way friars moved into areas close to old monasteries and began preaching and teaching to the local people.

ABOVE *St Francis made a profound impact on his contemporaries. His belief in the importance of absolute poverty was controversial. Despite this, Pope Innocent gave him permission to establish an approved religious order. This painting by the great Italian artist, Giotto, shows Francis and his early followers with the Pope*

◆ ON THE INSOLENCE OF THE FRANCISCANS: At this time some of the Franciscans impudently entered the territories of some noble monasteries under the pretence of fulfilling their duties of preaching, as if intending to depart after preaching the next day. Under pretence of sickness or on some other pretext, however, they remained. They said that they had permission from the Pope to hear confessions .... They broke forth in insults and threats, reviling every order except their own, and asserting that all the rest were amongst those doomed to damnation. *(Matthew Paris)*

One of the most exciting thinkers of the thirteenth century was the English Franciscan, Roger Bacon. Working in Oxford and Paris, Bacon pioneered the use of experimentation as a means of testing scientific knowledge. He won an international reputation as a genius and wonder-worker. Some of his admirers exaggerated his power; one claimed that he created a bridge from England to the Continent 'by the condensation of air'.

Women were also attracted to the teachings of Francis and Dominic. However, Church law banned women from preaching

RIGHT *An imagined scene, dating from the thirteenth century, showing friars and lay people during the final days before the Second Coming of Christ*

ABOVE *A Franciscan friar hears confession from a Franciscan nun, or 'Poor Clare'. Unlike the friars, Franciscan nuns lived a life of strict seclusion*

ABOVE *Roger Bacon, an English Franciscan and one of the greatest scientists of the Middle Ages*

The arrival of the friars coincided with the rise of the new universities. No longer were the established monasteries the only major centres of learning. The monks took some time to come to terms with the universities. By contrast, the friars immediately allied themselves to the new colleges in Oxford, Cambridge and Paris. Several leading university lecturers became friars and they soon came to dominate the teaching in the university schools. The friars were beginning to replace the monks as the intellectual leaders of the Christian world, and they wielded great influence: the Franciscan Adam Marsh was not only a famous university teacher but also a leading adviser to King Henry III. The Italian Dominican, Thomas Aquinas, revolutionised the teaching of philosophy and his writings came to dominate the subject for centuries.

and neither order allowed women to share in the wandering mission of the friars. Although Franciscan and Dominican orders were established for women, they were little different from the older orders: the nuns were obliged to spend all their time within the precincts of the convent. Eventually about 190 friaries for men were established in medieval England, but in the same period only one Dominican and five Franciscan convents for women were founded. One of these, the Franciscan house at Aldgate in London, was supported by many aristocratic and royal ladies. Its patrons included Queen Isabella, the turbulent wife of Edward II. Together with her lover, the Earl of Mortimer, Isabella played a part in the gruesome murder of her husband. According to one tradition, she later repented and joined the Franciscan order before her death.

ABOVE *Because friaries were usually built in cities, there are relatively few remains of medieval Franciscan and Dominican architecture. One exception is Blackfriars, the Dominican convent in Gloucester*

DECLINE AND FALL

The monasteries of England were closed down in the sixteenth century. The years before the dissolution were, in general terms, a period of decline for monasticism. The high standards of the early monasteries were frequently allowed to lapse, although some religious orders maintained to the end a reputation for dedication and holiness.

THE GOOD LIFE

ABOVE *A carved wooden boss from the roof of the fifteenth-century refectory at Cleeve Abbey, Somerset. The early Cistercians had rejected decoration and chosen an architectural style of great simplicity. This ornate roof boss is quite out of keeping with the initial idealistic principles of the order*

BELOW *The church of Mount Grace Priory, North Yorkshire. This strict Carthusian community was established in 1398*

There was a general decline in monastic fervour during the later Middle Ages. Relatively few new monasteries were established and the standard of discipline deteriorated in many places. The slackness of this period was reflected in the widespread practice of providing regular wages and holidays for monks and nuns. Despite frequent condemnation by the authorities, it became common for monks and nuns to receive money for the purchase of clothes and spices. In 1421 a meeting of the abbots of English Benedictine monasteries admitted defeat and sanctioned the paying of wages. Many monasteries designated a particular manor house as a holiday home for members of the community. By the fifteenth century almost every Benedictine house possessed a holiday home and each monk could expect an annual visit. Some monks and nuns even took holidays with friends and relatives. It also became increasingly common for monks and nuns to abandon the common dormitory in favour of private rooms.

Proof that monks and nuns were now paid wages can be found in the custom of fining them for breaches of rules. In 1432 at Ramsey Abbey in Cambridgeshire monks were fined 6d for drinking after the service of compline.

There were, however, some monks and nuns in the later Middle Ages who maintained the highest possible standards. Certain orders, renowned for holiness, continued to expand. The austere Carthusian order flourished, for example, the number of Carthusian houses in England increasing from two to nine. The Carthusians were patronised by the royal family, as was a strict branch of the Franciscans known as the Observants.

Henry V established a large Charterhouse (as Carthusian houses were known) at Richmond in Surrey. At nearby Syon he founded a fervent monastery of the new Bridgettine order. Saintliness among the Carthusians is evidenced by the life of Richard Methley, a monk of Mount Grace Priory in Yorkshire. Methley was born in about 1451 and became a Carthusian at the age of twenty-five. He had an intense spiritual life and wrote extensively about his mystical experiences. In one autobiographical work he describes his prayers and contemplations in the autumn of 1487:

SCENE FROM A CARTHUSIAN LIFE: AUGUST 1487
On the feast of St Peter in Chains I was in the church at Mount Grace, and after celebrating Mass was engaged in thanksgiving in prayer and meditation, when God visited me in

ABOVE *A fourteenth-century incense boat and censer from Ramsey Abbey, Cambridgeshire. The great wealth of the larger monastic houses allowed them to purchase precious and costly adornments for their churches. These elaborately ornamented objects were made from silver. The 'boat' was a container for ritual incense, and the censer was used for burning the incense*

The abbot's great hall at Battle Abbey, Sussex. By the sixteenth century many abbots and abbesses had abandoned the earlier practice of sharing sleeping quarters with the ordinary monks and nuns. Instead they built separate lodgings for themselves which were frequently fine enough to be adapted into secular manor houses after the dissolution

ABOVE *'Huby's Tower', at the Cistercian abbey of Fountains in Yorkshire, was built by Abbot Huby not long before the destruction of the monasteries. In the twelfth century Bernard of Clairvaux had criticised the Cluniacs for their love of luxurious architectural detail; he would certainly have disapproved of such an elaborate structure*

power, and I yearned with love so as almost to give up the ghost. Love and longing for the Beloved raised me in spirit into heaven. As the pain of love grew more powerful I could scarce have any thought at all, forming within my spirit these words: 'Love! Love! Love!'
(Richard Methley)

A WORLDLY PRIORESS

The laxness in some monastic houses is indicated in the reports written after episcopal visitations or inspections. One surviving report dates from 1441, when the Bishop of Lincoln visited Ankerwyke Priory, a Benedictine nunnery in Buckinghamshire. Clemence Medforde, the prioress, was accused of a series of extravagant breaches of the rules on clothing. She wore expensive gold rings with an assortment of precious stones. Her girdles were decorated with silver and gilt. She wore a silk veil and her shifts were made of expensive French cloth. Her 'kirtle' or outer gown was 'laced with silk' and she had a fur cap.

Few of the sisters had a kind word for the prioress. The bishop was told that six nuns had abandoned the monastic life and left the priory while she was in charge. Clemence herself was criticiscd for leaving the priory for social outings, such as a visit to a wedding. While the prioress indulged herself in matters of fashion, the other nuns were extremely badly clothed. The chief accuser, a nun named Margery Kirkby, said of the prioress, 'She furnishes not, nor for three years' space has furnished, fitting habits to the nuns, insomuch as the nuns go about in patched clothes'. Margery accused Clemence of blocking a window that gave the sisters a fine view over the River Thames. Clemence replied that she had blocked the window 'because she saw that men stood in the narrow space close to the window and talked with the nuns'.

The visit of the bishop must have been a traumatic experience for the incompetent and unpopular prioress. A year later Clemence was dead and her enemy, Margery Kirkby, had taken her place as prioress. Whether or not Margery unblocked the window is not known.

BELOW *An illustration of Dante's* Inferno, *dating from about 1400. A crowd of monks and a priest are damned for their sins. Evidence shows that some late medieval monasteries had lapsed into immoral ways; others continued to set high standards of piety and dedication to the monastic ideal*

DISSOLUTION

In the 1530s, during the reign of Henry VIII, the monastic houses of England and Wales were swept away. The dissolution of the monasteries was part of the wider European Reformation. Continental Protestant leaders, such as Martin Luther and John Calvin, established a new 'reformed' Christianity which rejected many of the traditional teachings of the Roman Catholic Church, including monasticism. Their teachings soon began to spread to England. Although Henry VIII had little sympathy for the attack on Catholic traditions, his marital problems led him to consider an independent Church in England. When at last he had given up hope of obtaining a divorce from the Pope, Henry declared himself Supreme Head of the Church in England. In 1534 monks and nuns were required to take an oath accepting Henry's new status. The great majority complied, but a few, including some leading Carthusians, objected and were executed.

There were signs of further trouble for monks and nuns in 1535. Henry's chief minister, Thomas Cromwell, organised an ominous valuation of all Church property, including monastic wealth. Cromwell sympathised with many Protestant ideas and was no friend of monasticism. He ordered a national visitation in 1535–36, to identify those monastic houses where there was abuse and poor discipline. The visitation came up with a result that suited Cromwell: its findings were that there was a high level of misconduct in the monasteries. After the visitation the government passed an act of Parliament closing down all those monastic communities with an income of £200 a year or less.

ABOVE *Henry VIII depicted in an initial letter, from the document containing the national valuation of all church property ordered by Cromwell in 1535. With a clear idea of the available booty as a result of this survey, Cromwell was better able to carry out the closure of the monasteries*

THE PILGRIMAGE OF GRACE

In much of the country the dissolution took place peacefully and, apparently, without much opposition. It appears that there was some support for the threatened monasteries in remote rural areas, especially in northern England. In 1536 an armed rebellion took place in Lincolnshire and Yorkshire, known as the Pilgrimage of Grace. The motives of the rebels were mixed but some of them were angry about the attack on the monasteries. The rebellion was eventually suppressed and its leaders put to death. Before his execution one of the leaders, a Lincolnshire lawyer named Robert Aske, paid a moving testimony to the work of the monks of northern England:

❖ The abbeys in the north parts gave great alms to poor men and laudably served God. By occasion of the suppression, the divine service of almighty God is much diminished. Many of the abbeys were in the mountains and desert places, where the people be rude of condition and not well taught the law of God, and when the abbeys stood the said people had not only worldly refreshing in their bodies but also spiritual refuge. None was in these parts denied so that the people were greatly refreshed by the said abbeys, where they now have no such succour. Also the abbeys were one of the beauties of this realm to all men and strangers passing through. Such abbeys as were near the sea were great maintainers of sea walls and dykes.

ABOVE *The Benedictine house of St Augustine's, Canterbury in about 1500. This reconstruction drawing gives a good impression of the scale of an important monastery a few years before the dissolution*

BELOW *The ruins of St Augustine's, Canterbury today. The history of this monastery went back to the earliest days of English monasticism, almost 1000 years before the dissolution*

VIVAT REX

Former inmates of monasteries were usually awarded pensions. These payments were honoured by successive governments and a few people were still in receipt of pensions after 1600, decades after the closure of their religious house.

THE FATE OF THE FORMER MONKS AND NUNS

The lives of those evicted from monasteries were extremely varied. The average pension for monks was about £5 per year. This was not enough to finance a luxurious lifestyle: it probably ensured subsistence, but little more. Payments to ex-friars were, in general, less generous than those made to former monks. The government hoped that both monks and friars would supplement any payments with additional earned income. There was no system for reducing payments if pensioners found paid employment. Many men obtained work ministering to parishes of the new Church of England. Opportunities for former nuns were much more restricted. For the younger nuns marriage was now an option. A study of former nuns in Lincolnshire indicated that, in that county, about 30 per cent married after the dissolution.

Former abbots were considerably better treated than were ordinary monks. In addition to a pension, an abbot or abbess could also expect to be given a house. The most generous of pensions were very lavish. The abbess of Shaftesbury received £133 a year. The abbot of Bury St Edmunds was paid £330. Sums of this kind were enough to support a life of considerable leisure and comfort.

THE END OF THE LARGE MONASTERIES

The closures of 1536 were only the beginning. All the remaining monasteries, including the larger institutions, were closed down between 1537 and 1540. Even before the monasteries were formally closed the great monastic shrines were destroyed and the jewels and treasure confiscated by the government. The last monastery to close was Waltham Abbey in Essex, which surrendered on 23 March 1540. Cromwell himself did not long outlive the monasteries he had destroyed. He fell out of favour with Henry and was executed in 1540.

THE LEGACY OF THE MONASTERIES

BELOW *Much beautiful art was destroyed at the time of the dissolution. This thirteenth-century carving of a monk from Winchester is a rare survival. It was hidden or lost during the destruction of the monasteries and only rediscovered in 1907. It had originally been part of the shrine of St Swithun. The shrines of important saints were destroyed early in the process of closing the monasteries*

ABOVE RIGHT *Winchester Cathedral Close. Winchester was one of eight monastic cathedrals that were transformed into communities of Anglican clergy. Many ex-monks obtained new jobs in these cathedrals*

After the dissolution the government set up a special organisation, the Court of Augmentations, to dispose of the monasteries and their estates. The confiscated monasteries and their lands were soon sold off, often to royal courtiers. Many of the church buildings were demolished almost immediately. Rapid demolition reduced the possibility that the monastery might one day be restored. The new owners sometimes built themselves handsome mansions out of the remains of the monastic buildings. In a few cases the families who acquired the former monastery have continued to live there up to the present day.

The scale of destruction varied from place to place. In some instances the demolition was so thorough that hardly a single stone of a massive complex of buildings now remains above ground. In other cases, the monastic church and cloister buildings have largely survived. There was a brief revival of monastic life under Mary Tudor (1553–58), who was anxious to reverse the religious changes brought about by Henry VIII and Edward VI. Only a handful of monasteries were reopened, however. Shortly after Mary's death, Elizabeth I showed her contempt for monasticism during a visit to Westminster Abbey. On being greeted by monks carrying large candles, she remarked: 'Away with those torches for we see very well'. The monastery was closed soon afterwards and the abbot sent to the Tower of London.

A small number of monks and nuns fled to the Continent to maintain their monastic life in exile. In practice most orders had ceased to function as international organisations by the sixteenth century and it was very difficult for English refugees to find a welcome abroad. Some Carthusians, Dominicans and Franciscans did make their way to Continental Europe and find new monastic homes. The Bridgettine convent of Syon emigrated as a community and, remarkably and uniquely, has continued in existence to the present day. Within a few years English Benedictines were established in exile.

SURVIVORS

Some monastic churches were left substantially intact for use as cathedrals, and in the process a number of jobs were preserved for redundant monks. Eight monasteries which had also functioned as cathedrals before the Reformation continued to exist solely as cathedrals: Canterbury, Rochester, Winchester, Ely, Norwich, Worcester, Durham and Carlisle. Monks were often kept on to serve as the clergy for the new non-monastic cathedrals. In addition, the government took advantage of the existence of former monasteries to create new cathedrals and bishoprics in Gloucester, Chester, Peterborough, Bristol and Oxford. Again, many ex-monks were retained to provide the

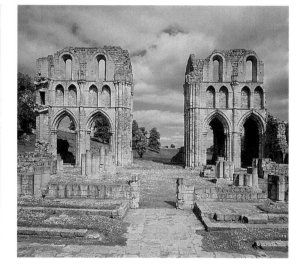

RIGHT *The overgrown ruins of Lindisfarne Priory, painted in 1796–97 by Thomas Girtin. By this time strong anti-Catholic feeling was abating and ruined medieval sites, including monasteries, were beginning to take on a romantic appeal*

ABOVE *The ruins of the monastic church at Roche Abbey, Yorkshire. In many places, such as the Cistercian community at Roche, the purchasers of the abbey immediately destroyed the church and cloisters so that there could be no possibility of re-establishing the monastic way of life*

ABOVE *Bury St Edmunds had been one of the richest and most powerful of monasteries. The monastic church was largely ruined but a fragment was reused as a house*

LEFT *Former monastic buildings were often turned into farm buildings. This farmhouse was once part of Halesowen Abbey in the West Midlands*

LEFT *A fragment of Pershore Abbey in Hereford and Worcester, now serving as the parish church for the town. Benedictine and Augustinian monasteries were often situated in towns and large villages, and, after the dissolution, could be purchased by the townsfolk for their parish church*

ABOVE *The ruins of Jervaulx Abbey in Yorkshire. Because of their remote setting most Cistercian houses could not be adapted to new functions and fell into ruin. Eventually these rural ruins became fashionable features of the landscape. At Jervaulx a nineteenth-century park was created around the remains of the monastery*

clergy. The creation of the new cathedrals also saved some distinguished architecture from destruction. The cloisters at Gloucester, for example, are widely considered to be the finest in the country.

NEW PARISH CHURCHES

The monastic churches of some abbey buildings were bought by the local people in order to be reused as parish churches. In many towns there was a long-standing tradition that the people of the parish should have the use of part of a local monastic church, often the nave. This explains why, after the dissolution, in towns such as Malmesbury, only the nave of the former abbey church was retained for parochial use. In a few cases, as at St Albans and Tewkesbury, almost the whole of the magnificent monastic church was transformed into a parish church. The surviving buildings were often Benedictine or Augustinian because these orders had a substantial presence in cities and towns. The great rural abbeys of the Cistercian order were more likely to be ruined.

It was only in the late eighteenth and early nineteenth centuries that anti-Roman Catholic discrimination in England was relaxed, allowing monks and nuns to return to England. The Benedictines established important abbeys and leading Catholic public schools at Downside and Ampleforth. Since their return, the religious orders have played an important part in the life of the Roman Catholic Church. Cardinal Basil Hume, the leader of the Catholic community in England, was abbot of Ampleforth before he became archbishop of Westminster.

⬡ ABBOTSBURY ABBEY, Dorset: Benedictine monks. The surviving buildings include the abbey gatehouse, a mill and barn.

⬡ BATTLE ABBEY *(above)*, Sussex: Benedictine monks. Part of the site is in English Heritage's care; part is now a private school. The ruined walls of the church and chapter house survive. Other remains include a fine gatehouse and precinct wall.

⬡ BAYHAM ABBEY, Sussex: Premonstratensian canons. Ruins of the church, cloister buildings and gatehouse.

⬡ BINHAM PRIORY, Norfolk: Benedictine monks. The surviving Norman nave of the monastic church is in use as a parish church. There are ruins of the rest of the church and the cloister buildings.

BOLTON PRIORY, North Yorkshire: Augustinian canons. The thirteenth-century nave of the monastic church survives as a parish church. The gatehouse is incorporated into a later house.

⬡ BOXGROVE PRIORY, Sussex: Benedictine monks. The parish church retains the chancel and transepts from the monastic church; most of the nave is ruined. A particularly fine example of Early English architecture.

⬡ BURY ST EDMUNDS ABBEY, Suffolk: Benedictine monks. The ruins of the abbey church lie in a public park. The magnificent Norman gateway survives intact.

⬡ BYLAND ABBEY *(above)*, North Yorkshire: Cistercian monks. Extensive ruins

of the church and cloisters survive. There is a good collection of architectural material in the site museum.

⬡ CANTERBURY, ST AUGUSTINE'S ABBEY, Kent: Benedictine monks. The ruins include both Saxon and Norman church buildings. Some buildings, including the abbot's house, have been incorporated into a private school.

CANTERBURY CATHEDRAL PRIORY, Kent: Benedictine monks. The monastic cloisters, chapter house and church survive intact as part of the cathedral. The choir was built in the late twelfth century to house the shrine of Becket. The nave, transepts and central tower were rebuilt in the fourteenth century.

CARLISLE CATHEDRAL, Cumbria: Augustinian canons. The church has an unusual layout, with a very short nave and an elongated choir. Carlisle was the only medieval cathedral to be served by Augustinian canons.

CHESTER CATHEDRAL, Cheshire: Benedictine monks. Extensive surviving monastic buildings include cloisters, chapter house and fine thirteenth-century refectory. The enormous south transept of the church served as the medieval parish church.

⬡ CLEEVE ABBEY *(above)*, Somerset: Cistercian monks. There are extensive remains of the cloister buildings, including a fifteenth-century refectory with a fine oak roof and unusual wall paintings in the abbot's lodging.

⬡ CREAKE ABBEY, Norfolk: Augustinian canons. The ruins of part of the church and cloister buildings survive.

CROWLAND ABBEY, Lincolnshire: Benedictine monks. The north aisle of the monastic church has survived as the parish church.

⬡ DENNY ABBEY, Cambridgeshire: Benedictine monks, Knights Templar and Franciscan nuns. The ruined abbey church has been incorporated into a later farmhouse. The refectory of the Franciscan nuns survives as a barn.

DORCHESTER ABBEY, Oxfordshire: Augustinian canons. The monastic church substantially survives as a parish church. It includes some medieval wall paintings. The other monastic buildings have been destroyed.

DURHAM CATHEDRAL PRIORY, Durham: Benedictine monks. The monastic church at Durham is the finest Norman building in England. The monks of Durham looked after the shrine of St Cuthbert. The cloisters survive, although they were modified in the eighteenth century. Other surviving monastic buildings include the dormitory, which is now a museum.

⬡ EASBY ABBEY, North Yorkshire: Premonstratensian canons. Surviving ruins include the gatehouse and cloister buildings. The church has been destroyed.

⬡ EGGLESTONE ABBEY, Durham: Premonstratensian canons. A later house incorporates part of the monastic church. Further parts of the church and cloister buildings exist in ruined form.

ELY CATHEDRAL, Cambridgeshire: Benedictine monks. The abbey church contains a unique central octagon. Fine Norman work in the nave.

FOUNTAINS ABBEY, North Yorkshire: Cistercian monks. The most extensive monastic ruins in England include substantial cloister buildings, a mill, gatehouse and several precinct buildings.

⬡ FURNESS ABBEY, Cumbria: Savigniac and later Cistercian monks. The ruined church and cloister buildings are well preserved. The distinctive Cistercian gatehouse chapel survives.

⬡ GISBOROUGH PRIORY *(above)*, Cleveland: Augustinian canons. Ruins of the church and cloister buildings.

GLASTONBURY ABBEY, Somerset: Benedictine monks. Substantial ruins of the church and cloister buildings. The abbot's kitchen has survived remarkably intact.

⬡ GLOUCESTER BLACKFRIARS, Gloucestershire: Dominican friars. Unusual survival of the church and cloister buildings of an urban friary. Later converted into a house and a factory.

GLOUCESTER CATHEDRAL, Gloucestershire: Benedictine monks. The abbey at Gloucester was transformed into a cathedral at the dissolution and many of the monastic buildings have survived. The chancel of the monastic church was transformed in the fourteenth century and contains some Perpendicular work of great beauty. The monastic cloisters are extremely well preserved and are, perhaps, the finest in England.

GREAT MALVERN PRIORY, Hereford and Worcester: Benedictine monks. The monastic church survived almost intact as a parish church. There is an unusual quantity of medieval stained glass and tiles.

✠ **HAILES ABBEY,** Gloucestershire: Cistercian monks. Ruined remains of monastic church and cloister buildings. The Cistercian gatehouse chapel survives as a parish church.

✠ **HAUGHMOND ABBEY,** Shropshire: Augustinian canons. Ruins of the cloister buildings and the abbot's hall.

JARROW PRIORY, Tyne and Wear: Benedictine monks. The home of Bede. The monastic church includes substantial Saxon work. The cloister buildings survive in a ruined state.

✠ **KIRKHAM PRIORY,** North Yorkshire: Augustinian canons. Ruins include a well-preserved gatehouse and cloister buildings.

KIRKSTALL ABBEY, West Yorkshire: Cistercian monks. Substantial ruins survive of church and cloister buildings. Other remains include the guesthouse and a gatehouse.

LACOCK ABBEY, Wiltshire: Augustinian nuns. A later house incorporates substantial elements of the cloister buildings.

✠ **LANERCOST PRIORY,** Cumbria: Augustinian canons. The nave of the monastic church survives intact as a parish church. Substantial further remains include part of the cloister and the prior's apartments.

LEOMINSTER PRIORY, Hereford and Worcester: Benedictine monks. The nave of the monastic church survives intact as a parish church.

✠ **LILLESHALL ABBEY,** Shropshire: Augustinian canons. Substantial remains of the church and cloister buildings.

✠ **LINDISFARNE PRIORY,** Northumberland: Benedictine monks. The monastery of St Cuthbert, although nothing remains of the Saxon work. Substantial ruins of fourteenth-century church and cloister buildings.

MALMESBURY ABBEY, Wiltshire: Benedictine monks. Part of the nave of the monastic church survives as a parish church. Remains include a magnificent Norman porch.

✠ **MONK BRETTON PRIORY,** South Yorkshire: Cluniac, later Benedictine monks. Extensive ruins of the church and cloister buildings. Surviving buildings include a gatehouse and mill.

✠ **MOUNT GRACE PRIORY,** North Yorkshire: Carthusian monks. The most substantial remains in the country of a Carthusian monastery. The ruins include a small church and inner and outer cloisters.

✠ **NETLEY ABBEY,** Hampshire: Cistercian monks. Well-preserved ruins of church and cloister buildings.

NORTON PRIORY, Cheshire: Augustinian canons. Ruins of church and cloister buildings have been recently excavated.

NORWICH CATHEDRAL, Norfolk: Benedictine monks. Surviving cloisters and chapter house. Magnificent Norman tower.

PETERBOROUGH CATHEDRAL, Cambridgeshire: Benedictine monks. Magnificent monastic church survives as the cathedral. Further surviving monastic buildings include abbot's lodging reused as the bishop's palace.

PERSHORE ABBEY, Hereford and Worcester: Benedictine monks. The chancel, crossing and south transept survive intact as a parish church.

✠ **RIEVAULX ABBEY,** North Yorkshire: Cistercian monks. Substantial ruins of the church and cloister buildings. Surviving buildings include a mill, tannery and gatehouse chapel.

✠ **ROCHE ABBEY,** South Yorkshire: Cistercian monks. Ruins of the church and cloister buildings.

ROCHESTER CATHEDRAL, Kent: Benedictine monks. This small monastic cathedral lies close to a Norman castle. The abbey church has a Norman nave and rare thirteenth-century furniture.

ROMSEY ABBEY, Hampshire: Benedictine nuns. The monastic church at Romsey was transformed into a parish church. The church is substantially Norman and the finest surviving example of a nuns' church.

✠ **SALLEY ABBEY,** Lancashire: Cistercian monks. Ruins of the church and cloister buildings.

✠ **SHAP ABBEY,** Cumbria: Premonstratensian canons. Ruins of the church and cloister buildings.

ST ALBANS CATHEDRAL, Hertfordshire: Benedictine monks. The extremely long abbey church contains a fine set of thirteenth- and fourteenth-century wall paintings.

✠ **THORNTON ABBEY** (below left), Humberside: Augustinian canons. Substantial remains of the walls and moat of the abbey. Magnificent gatehouse, possibly the finest surviving monastic gatehouse in England.

✠ **TITCHFIELD ABBEY,** Hampshire: Premonstratensian canons. The nave of the church survives as part of a later mansion.

✠ **WALTHAM ABBEY,** Essex: Augustinian canons. The Norman nave survives as a parish church. There are a late fourteenth-century gatehouse and part of the cloister.

✠ **WENLOCK PRIORY,** Shropshire: Cluniac monks. Ruins of the church and cloister buildings. Remains include the prior's house and the infirmary.

✠ **WESTMINSTER ABBEY,** London: Benedictine monks. The abbey church was substantially rebuilt by Henry III in the thirteenth century. A number of other surviving monastic buildings include the octagonal chapter house.

✠ **WAVERLEY ABBEY,** Surrey: Cistercian monks. The first Cistercian house in England. There are slight remains of the church and cloister buildings.

✠ **WHITBY ABBEY** (above), North Yorkshire: Benedictine monks. Substantial ruins of the monastic church. Part of the abbot's house is incorporated into a later house.

WINCHESTER CATHEDRAL, Hampshire: Benedictine monks. The cathedral was taken over by Benedictine monks during the monastic revival of the tenth century. The abbey church is now the longest cathedral in England.

WORCESTER CATHEDRAL, Hereford and Worcester: Benedictine monks. Worcester was one of the dual-purpose monasteries and cathedrals that were a unique feature of the English medieval Church. The monastic remains include the church and fine crypt, a round chapter house and cloisters.

YORK ABBEY, North Yorkshire: Benedictine monks. An unusual survival is the fortified wall of the monastic precinct, including three gates. The ruins of the church and other buildings, including the abbot's lodging and guesthouse, also remain.

✠ *Sites in the care of English Heritage. Telephone 0171 973 3434 for details.*

INDEX

ACKNOWLEDGEMENTS. English Heritage would like to thank:

Dr Glyn Coppack and Nick Kavanagh for advice; Terry Ball, Tracey Croft, Peter Dunn, Judith Dobie, Simon Hayfield, David Honour, Margaret Mahoney and Jim Thorn for permission to reproduce their illustrations.

The following books have been quoted extensively in the text: *The Monastic Constitutions of Lanfranc*, ed and trans David Knowles (Nelson, 1951); *The Rule of St Benedict*, ed and trans Justin McCann (Sheed & Ward, 1972); Bede, *A History of the English Church and People*, trans Leo Sherley-Price (Penguin, 1955); *The Chronicles of Matthew Paris*, ed and trans Richard Vaughan (Sutton Publishing, 1986); *The Chronicle of Jocelin of Brakelond*, ed H E Butler (Nelson, 1949); and *The Peasants' Revolt of 1381*, ed R B Dobson (Macmillan, 1970).

Picture credits:

Aerofilms 50 tl, 61 cr; **AKG** 24 r, 27 l, 26 tl; **Antiquities Museum, Stockholm** 34 tl; **Bede Centre/Peter Dunn** 30; **Bergen University Museum** 34 c; **British Library** 31 r, 41 tr, 42 br, (Harley 3244 f28) 5, (Harley 3244 f28) 13 bl, (Add 18192 f110) 8 r, (Add 18192 f110) 8 bl, (Add 33247) 46 cr, (Add 37049 f22/23) 12, (Add 39943) 31 bl, (Add 39943 f21) 7 br, (Add 39943 f39) 18 c, (Add 42130 f202) 47 cr, (Add 42130 f202v) 40 bl, (Add 42130 f87v) 43 br, (Arundel 155 f133) 27 tr, (Claud B iv f19) 35 l, (Cotton Dom Axvii 49v) 26 bl, (Cotton Claud EIV f124) 23 br, (Cotton Dom AVII f150v) 39 r, (Cotton Dom Axvii f73v) 6, (Cotton Vesp A V111) 35 c, (Cotton Vit AXIII f6v) 53 c, (Harley 5102 f87) 49 t, (Harley 1498 f76) 16 l, (Harley 1527 f33v) 14 cr, (Harley 5431 f6v-7) 27 c, (Harley Roll Y6) 14 l, (Roy 18 D11 f148) 49 br, (Royal 10E 4 f187v) 14 br, (Royal 14C VII) 22 bl, (Royal 14C VII f5v) 22 r,
(Royal 20E 1 f175) 50 r, (Royal 2B IV f24v) 9 l, (Royal GVI) 44 t, (Soane 4235 f44v) 7 c, (Yates Thompson 11) 15; **British Museum** 30 l, 32 l, 33 tl, 61 l; **Bodleian Library, Oxford** (Ms 211 f5) 55 l, (Ms 264 f79r) 54 l, (Ashmole 1431 f20r), 23 cl (Auct D 2 6 f4r) 42 tr, (Auct F 4 32) 35 br, (Ch Suff a 1 No5) 51 cl, (Douce 180 p35/16/11/95) 55 c, (Douce 131 f126r) 55 r, (Junius 11 p 13) 33 br, (Laud Misc 385 f41v) 23 tr, (Laud Misc 385 f41v) 24 tl, (Laud Misc 385 f41v) 24 c, 16 t, (Ms 569 f1r) 37 bl, (Ms Top Gloucs d 2) 46 b, (Douce 366 f9v) 21; **Burrell Collection** 49 cr; **CADW** (D M Robinson, *Tintern Abbey*, 3rd edn, 1995) 10 l & 19; **Cambridge University Library** (Ms Ee 359 f37) 48 l; **Corpus Christi College, Cambridge** (Ms 10 f181r) 40 tl, (Ms 26 f18r) 9 tr, (Ms 16 f216r) 48 b, (Ms 180 f1r) 13 tr, (Ms 16 f93r) 12 l, (Ms 16 f53v) 25 tl; **Corpus Christi College, Oxford** (Ms157 p382) 52 b; **John Critchley** 61 br; **Dijon Bibliothèque Municipale** 8 tl, 39 tl, 41 bl, 7 l; **Durham Cathedral** 31 cl; **Edifice** 60 cl; **ET Archive** 45 br, 47 cl, 54 r; **Fotomas** 22 tl; **Giraudon/Chantilly Museum** 57 b; **Sonia Halliday** front cover, 1, 14 tr, 26 r, 28 br, 44 br, 45 tr, 45 c; **Hatfield House** 50 b; **Heidelberg University Library** 28 tl; **Michael Holford** 36 tl, 36 cl; **A F Kersting** 44 bl, 52 l; **Museu de Palma** 38 br; **Museum of London** 49; **National Library of Scotland** 24 bl; **National Monuments Record** 20 tr; **National Museum of Scotland** 28 bl, 53 tr; **National Portrait Gallery** 46 cl, 59 r; **Pierpoint Morgan Library/Art Resource NY** (Ms 736 f19v) 51 t; **Public Record Office** 41 tl, 58 l; **Sidney Sussex College, Cambridge** 12 tr, 13; **St Johns College, Oxford** 23 cr; **Trinity College, Dublin** 18 l; **Trinity College, Cambridge** (Ms R.17.1 f284-5) 10; **Trinity Hall, Cambridge** (Ms1 f77r) 28 tr; **V&A** 17, 20, 1, 56 r; **Winchester Cathedral** 60 l; **Yorkshire Museum** 18 l, 20 br. All other photographs are the copyright of English Heritage (telephone 0171-973 3338 for details).

Every effort has been made to trace the copyright holders and we apologise in advance for any unintentional omissions, which we would be pleased to correct in any subsequent edition of this book.